E9m

D0297339

CENTRAL LIBRARY, MARKET SQUARE, PRESTON 53191

THE

LANCASHIRE

LIBRARY

PRESTON
LOCAL
STUDIES

AUTHOR	CLASS No.
BOOTH, J	525 C11
LOOKING AT OLD MAPS	PQ B465589952

This book must be returned on or before the date shown above
to the Library from which it was borrowed
LANCASHIRE COUNTY LIBRARY 4 3 81
143 CORPORATION STREET, PRESTON, PR1 8RH

Lancashire County Library

30118095550095

John Cary map of Somerset, Dorset and Devon (parts), 1794	£30
Laurie and Whittle plan of Fishguard Bay, 1797	?
John Cary map of Scotland, 1803 (1808)	£30
John Luffman map of Merionethshire, 1803	£60
Edward Mogg road map London to Exeter (part), 1814	£20
Langley and Belch map of Huntingdonshire, 1818	£30
Ordnance Survey map of Cardigan, 1819	£40
William Darton map of Buckinghamshire, 1822 (1833)	£40
Michel Perrot maps of (a) Aberdeen and Kincardine, 1823 (b) York, 1823	£30 and £40
Henry Teesdale map of South Wales, 1829 (1840)	£30
Pigot & Co., map of Monmouth, 1829 (1831)	£25
John and Christopher Greenwood map of Worcestershire, 1830	£40
Lt. Robert K. Dawson map of Bath, 1831	£15
John and Charles Walker map of North and South Wales, 1832	£12
Thomas Moule map of Isle of Man, 1836 (1843)	£20
Archibald Fullerton & Co., map of Devonshire, 1843	£20
Hugh Hughes map of North Wales, 1845	£100
Reuben Ramble map of Oxfordshire, 1845	£70
John Archer map of Cornwall, 1848	£15
John Tallis map of Ireland	£25
Caricature map of Wales — Vincent Brooks, Day & Son, c. 1870	£60

NOTES

The prices quoted are mean averages compiled from the current lists of five major map-dealers in the U.K. As every collector knows, there is no fixed price for a particular antique and much depends on how much the dealer paid and the margin of profit he expects. Prices quoted by dealers specialising in old maps are sometimes higher, but frequently lower, than maps purchased from other sources.

New industrial or other developments, e.g. North Sea Oil, county boundary changes, loss of county identity (the counties of Brecon, Radnor and Montgomeryshire no longer exist!) are all factors that influence prices. The future development of oil prospecting in S.W. England could bring British and foreign customers to the region who might well purchase old maps. Observe the high price now demanded for maps of Middle East oil producing countries.

British county maps are generally priced according to the size and importance of the county and the decorative merit of the map. For example a Speed of Cornwall is likely to be more than twice the price of say a Speed of Shropshire; the former map being at the top of the dealers' "League Table", the latter much lower down.

Looking at Old Maps 1979

Guide to Map Prices—Unframed

Humphrey Lhuyd map of England & Wales, Ortelius, 1573 (1579)	£400
Humphrey Lhuyd map of Wales, Ortelius, 1573	£400
Claudius Ptolemy map of the British Isles, Mercator, 1578	£600
Christopher Saxton map of Glamorganshire, 1578	£2,000
Petrus Bertius map of Great Britain, 1600 (1616)	£75
William Smith map of Surrey, 1600 (1670)	£600
William Camden map of Lancashire, 1607 (1637)	£120
John Speed map of Wiltshire, 1611 (1662)	£230
Michael Drayton map of Somerset/Wiltshire, 1612 (1613)	£120
Pieter Van den Keere map of Southampton (Hampshire) 1617 (1646)	£45
John Bill map of Wiltshire, 1626	£75
Jacob Van Langeren map of Wales, Simmons, 1635 (1643)	£50
Joan Blaeu map of Hampshire, 1645 (1648)	£200
Jan Jansson map of Ireland, 1646 (1659)	£200
Richard Blome map of Somerset, 1673	£70
John Ogilby road-map Oxford to Bristol, 1675 (1698)	£70
Excerpt from Ogilby Road Atlas, 1675	—
William Redmayne playing card map of Montgomeryshire, 1676 (1712)	£80
Captain Greenvile Collins chart of Milford Haven, 1693 (1723)	£160
John Seller map of Glamorganshire, 1695	£40
Robert Morden map of Ireland, 1695 (1722)	£60
Schenk and Valk issue of map of South Wales, 1646 (c. 1695)	£120
John Senex road-map Barnstaple to Truro (part II), 1719	£25
Thomas Gardner road-map Shrewsbury to Holiwell, 1719	£35
John Owen and Emanuel Bowen map of Lincolnshire, 1720	£25
Herman Moll map of Herefordshire, 1724	£40
Badeslade and Toms map of Middlesex, 1742	£25
Thomas Osborne map of Carnarvonshire, 1748	£20
Thomas Kitchin & Thomas Jefferys map of Gloucestershire, 1749	£25
Thomas Kitchin map of Haddingtonshire, 1750	£25
George Bickham Bird's Eye view of Warwickshire, 1750	£100
John Rocque map of Shropshire (parts), 1753	£60
G. Rollos map of Brecknockshire, 1760 (1768)	£25
John Ellis map of North Wales (verso South), 1766	£25
Emanuel and Thomas Bowen map of Durham, 1767	£45
Bowles's Reduced map of Anglesea Isle, 1785	?
Thomas Conder map of Cambridgeshire, 1786	£25
John Tuke map of Holderness, 1786 (1794)	£85

LOOKING AT OLD MAPS

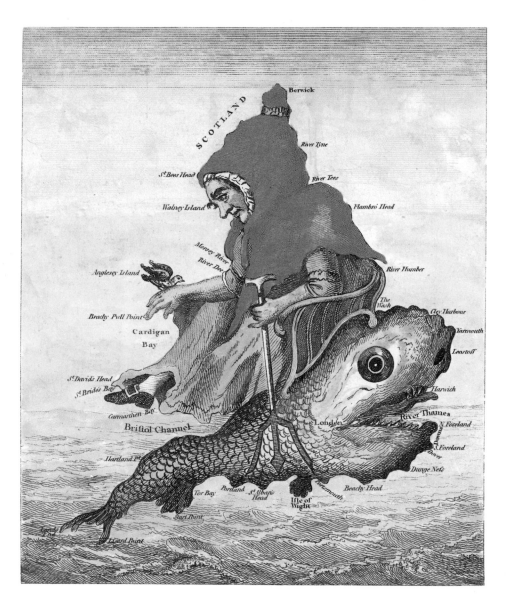

A Whimsical Representation of England and Wales.

Looking At Old Maps

John Booth

1979

CAMBRIDGE HOUSE BOOKS
WESTBURY, WILTSHIRE

FIRST EDITION

© John Booth 1979

ISBN 0 906853 00 1

00210767

465589952 PQ

Printed in Great Britain
by
The Blackmore Press
Shaftesbury, Dorset

"Great things are done when
Men and mountains meet—
These are not done by
Jostling in the Street"

William Blake

Contents

List of Map Illustrations

N.B. The first date is that of original edition the second, the date of the map illustrated.

Acknowledgements

My thanks are due to Miss Marion Barton, Mr. Bill Collins and my brother Tom for permission to reproduce maps from their collections. To Jonathan Potter for help with research on Map No 59, and to Barbara Pritchard for typing the manuscript.

I also wish to record appreciation for use of reference works by Mr. R. Vere Tooley and the late Dr. R. A. Skelton.

Author's Note

This is a book about old maps, a subject that has fascinated me for many years. In the pages that follow, the reader is introduced to some of the many British maps published over the past four hundred years, possibly the most exciting period in our long history.

Maps continue to play an important part in our daily lives, helping us towards a holiday destination or with the purchase of a home, where the conveyancing plan is usually taken from the Ordnance Survey. We take our modern maps for granted without a thought for previous generations of surveyors and engravers who made them possible.

I hope the book will interest the general reader and the intending collector by helping both towards a greater awareness and appreciation of our nation's cartographic heritage

John Booth

Westbury
Wiltshire
June, 1979

First Steps in Map Collecting

Map Sources

The first engraved atlas of the World based on the researches of Claudius Ptolemy of Alexandria (100-178 A.D.) was published at Bologna in Italy in 1477, but the term Atlas to describe a bound volume of maps was first used by Mercator a century later. Few maps of Britain are known before the famous fourteenth century Gough map now housed in the Bodlian Library of Oxford. George Lily, a Catholic refugee is thought to have been the originator of the first printed map of Britain published in 1547. This was followed in 1564 by a fine large scale map of the British Isles by Gerard Mercator of projection fame

The first printed map of England and Wales appeared in an Atlas of the World by Abraham Ortelius. Although this Atlas, *The Theatrum Orbis Terrarum*, was published in 1570 this map was not included until the edition of 1573. It was the work of a Welshman, Humphrey Lhuyd of Denbigh, whose map of Wales was also included. We look later, in greater detail at the major contribution made by Humphrey Lhuyd to British cartography.

The most famous map-maker of the Sixteenth Century was undoubtedly Gerard Mercator. He, like Ortelius, compiled an important World Atlas which he commenced to issue in parts in 1585 although the complete work was not finally published until after his death in 1594.

Mercator was a skilled engraver and personally engraved all the maps in his edition of *Ptolemy's Geography* published in 1578. He is regarded as the most important name in cartography after Ptolemy and his son and grandsons continued the family tradition. The atlases of Mercator and Ortelius ran to many editions and the maps they contained are now keenly sought by collectors throughout the world.

In Britain at about this time, Christopher Saxton was working on a County Atlas of England and Wales, the first national atlas of its kind to be produced anywhere in the world. Although individual maps from the Atlas had been issued prior to its publication in 1579, this fine work was to enjoy a long life and was republished many times during the next two hundred years.

The British challenge to the supremacy of continental map-makers was now established and various foreign engravers and publishers began to copy British maps. One of them, Pieter Van den Keere, engraved a series of miniature maps of the English and Welsh counties,

1

together with some of Ireland and Scotland. These date from the late 1500's. Had they been published in atlas form at that time, Keere would have been the first man to complete an atlas of the British Isles.

The great Elizabethan historian, William Camden, is thought to have been persuaded by Ortelius to illustrate his monumental work *Britannia* with maps of the English and Welsh counties. His 1607 edition was to include maps, copied from those of Saxton and Norden.

John Norden, a contemporary of Saxton, had hoped to emulate him by producing an updated atlas survey of the English counties and his were the first county maps to depict roads. Alas, financial difficulties thwarted his intentions and he only managed to produce manuscripts for twelve maps, few of which were printed in his life time. These Norden maps are much scarcer than their Saxton counterparts and are regarded by many collectors as superior in style and presentation.

William Smith was another important Elizabethan cartographer whose work is rarely found today. He is thought to have been responsible for about a dozen maps, formerly known as the Anonymous Series, most of which were copied from those of Saxton and Norden.

In the year 1611 John Speed's famous atlas *The Theatre of the Empire of Great Britain* was published, containing what are undoubtedly the best known of all British county maps. There was a continuing demand for this Atlas which remained in print until a final issue in 1770. Information about the particular county taken from Camden's *Britannia* is usually printed on the backs of these maps. Some pre-atlas issues and certain later reprints of the Atlas. (like the one published by Roger Rea in 1662) have plain backs. An example from Speed's Atlas would be a worthwhile addition to any collection but these maps are now becoming difficult to find and certain counties are very expensive.

Following the publication of Speed's Atlas came the Dutch challenge from the Blaeu and Jansson publishing houses. Most of the British maps they issued were copied from Saxton or Speed, but their high quality engraving and pleasing appearance quickly established their popularity with the nobility and gentry of Europe. A number of private libraries in this Country and abroad still contain fine examples, handed down over the centuries. Following the publication of Speed's Atlas in 1611, British county mapping entered a period of stagnation that was to last for the greater part of the century. The county atlases of Richard Blome and Robert Morden issued later were mainly copied from the earlier cartographers mentioned. Although Morden claimed that his maps were

2

revised and based on updated information, there appears little evidence to support this.

After Speed, the most important British map-making achievement of the seventeenth century was the publication of John Ogilby's *Britannia Road Atlas* in 1676, which contained one hundred maps detailing the principal roads of England and Wales. The improvement in roads and the development of the coaching system produced a demand for a new kind of map quite different from the road-less, decorative masterpieces of the previous century. It was this Atlas which doubtless inclined Morden to include roads on the maps in his County Atlas published some twenty years later. Other map-makers were quick to follow Morden's lead and many of the atlases that were produced in the early eighteenth century, paid increasing attention to roads.

Towards the end of the century, many more map publishers entered the market and the introduction of steel printing plates in the early eighteen hundreds enabled editions to be printed in thousands rather than the hundreds of the copper plate era.

Eighteenth and nineteenth century maps still provide an opportunity for the collector of modest means to assemble an interesting collection on a relatively small outlay. Certain examples, however, like the Luffman, Langley, Perrot and Ramble are an indication that rarity rather than age can frequently influence price. We now take a brief look at the way in which early maps were prepared and printed, as a little knowledge of the techniques involved can be helpful to the new collector.

Early Surveying

In sixteenth century Britain when a number of the maps reviewed in this book were first prepared survey methods were something of a hit-and-miss affair. About the year 1560, a new system known as triangulation was introduced and combined a magnetic compass with a sighting instrument called an alidade, which was used in conjunction with a sketching or plane-table. The surveyor worked from a vantage point on a hill or a church tower and built up a series of triangulated sketches of the surrounding countryside, measuring the distance between vantage points with a calibrated measuring wheel or way-wiser which travelled a distance of eight and a quarter feet per revolution. Poles, together with a measuring cord of known length were used for sighting and measuring. These rather basic items comprised the somewhat limited tools of the surveyor's trade in 1570 when Christopher Saxton started the first ever county by county survey of England and Wales.

Making the Printing Plate

After the survey work was complete, manuscript copies of the maps were passed to the engravers for incising onto sheets of copper, by a hand worked process known as line-engraving. The smooth rounded handle of the engraving tool (graver) was concealed in the palm of the hand and the point of the tool pushed forward and downwards into the surface of the copper plate, cutting a line or groove. The method called for great care and skill and was very time consuming, the work on a single plate taking many months to complete. The operation was further complicated by the fact that all the detail had to be engraved in reverse. If you attempt to write out, in reverse, all the place names on a particular map, you will gain some idea of the easy part of the engraver's task.

Method of Printing

When the engraving of the plate was complete, it passed to the printer. As ink was only required in the grooves, the plate could not be inked by a roller, as in letterpress printing, but was inked by hand using a dabber, which filled all the incised lines with ink. The plate's surface was wiped clean and rubbed with the ball of the palm to ensure that unwanted surface ink had been removed. After setting the plate in the press, printing was ready to commence.

Unlike present day methods, the process of cleaning off and re-inking the plate had to be repeated for each impression taken. Considerable pressure was required on the press in order to force the previously dampened paper into the grooved detail of the plate, although cleaning off and balling of the copper plate is thought to have been responsible for more plate wear than the action of the press. The press pressure caused

4

an indentation in the paper where it was in contact with the edges of the plate, producing a plate-mark. This plate-mark should be clearly visible on all old maps printed from copper plates.

The copper sheet used for plate-making in the sixteenth, seventeenth and eighteenth centuries, seldom exceeded one eighth of an inch in thickness and was very expensive to produce. For this reason, the engraver ordered his plate only fractionally larger than the outer border of the map. Generally speaking, the earlier the map the closer the platemark is to the map's border. If a map is dated, or known to have been produced before 1820 it should have a plate-mark, unless made from a woodblock or by lithographic means. Unfortunately, copper plate maps were sometimes trimmed to the edges of the map's border with subsequent loss of the plate-mark and sometimes the engraved surface, e.g. Drayton's Polyolbion. Such examples are usually rejected by the serious collector, the maps having lost something of their original condition.

Introduction of Steel Plates

By the mid eighteen twenties, soft steel was replacing copper for plate making. These new plates were much harder than copper and whereas a copper plate would begin to show signs of wear after about three hundred impressions, steel plates would print well in excess of twenty times that number without any marked loss of definition. Fine line work was possible on this harder metal and material costs were much lower. Needless to say, the engraver's began to use plates quite a bit larger than the engraved surface of the map and plate marks several inches away from the map's border were not uncommon. Frequently, the surrounding paper margins were trimmed before maps were bound and the plate mark was lost.

From the foregoing, it will be appreciated that the quality of the printing of early maps made from copper plates can vary a great deal, depending on the age and condition of the plate and on the ability of the printer. The high cost and special engraving skill demanded in the production of John Speed's rare county map plates, published in 1611, saw them still in use twelve editions and one hundred and sixty years later. Some atlases, like the Speed, were re-issued many times, others not at all. Information on a map's issues is of great importance to the discriminating collector.

Paper and Watermarks

Now a word about the paper used in the production of early maps, for it provides the expert, by its feel and appearance, with final proof of a map's authenticity. Until the 1700's much of the paper used in Britain was imported from the Continent.

Publishers often borrowed plates in order to make up an atlas and at the same time, had to use paper of sufficient size to accommodate the largest map to be printed. As a result there were often variations in the size of maps in the same atlas, the smaller ones being surrounded by wide margins. Good examples of this can be found in the *English Atlas* of Moses Pitt, where some maps have six inch margins. In the case of Speed and Blaeu, the dimensions of the maps were fairly constant although most editions of Speed's maps are found with narrow margins. The Blaeus', on the other hand, enhanced the presentation of their atlases with wide margins, which apart from looking more attractive, reduced the chances of damage to individual maps by constant handling.

If you hold a map made before about 1780 up to the light a series of parallel lines about one and a quarter inches apart become visible. When the paper was being made, the individual sheets were placed in wire lined trays to dry and the mark made by the wire became incorporated into the paper. Paper-makers took advantage of this and built designs into the bottom of the trays made of soldered wire, thus identifying each sheet of paper they made. Of course, this device would date only the paper, not the map, since printers often used existing stocks of paper to print items published at a later date. Wire marks are rarely found on papers after the late 1700's when the method of manufacture was changed.

Later papers tend to be whiter, finer in surface texture, and sometimes thicker than their earlier counterparts and contain increasing quantities of size to give the paper more body and provide a better printing surface. Little difficulty is experienced in hand colouring on paper of this kind. On the other hand, old papers are highly absorbent, designed to attract ink at the printing stage. An attempt to apply colour to an old map without the knowledge and skill of a professional colourist is to court disaster, unless one is able to colour to fine limits on blotting paper!

Some of the maps in the collection carry date watermarks, which are particularly useful. I have just been looking at a small Cary map of Wiltshire with a publisher's imprint of 1787. After congratulating myself on finding a first edition in mint condition, I held the map to the light, only to discover an 1802 dated watermark.

It would seem that marking paper by means of watermarks has been in use since the fourteenth century and, of course, the practice is still with us today. The first British paper-maker was a John Tate of Stevenage, some of whose paper was used to print Caxton's works, but Sir John Spielman of Dartford (fl.1588-1605) is the better known and was responsible for introducing the Jester's cap and bells or Fool's cap watermark. Many different designs are used and some of the earliest marks were often religious in origin incorporating variations of the Cross as well as Pascal Lamb, Crozier and Cardinal's Hat. Armorial devices were popular, sometimes surmounted by a crown; as were mythological birds and animals, weaponry, flowers and fruit. Several watermarks later gave their names to British paper sizes, of which 'Crown' and 'Foolscap' are probably the better known.

During the sixteenth and seventeenth centuries, much of the paper used by British printers was imported from the Continent and either of Dutch, German or French origin. The great name in British paper making is that of James Whatman, whose Turkey Mill at Maidstone flourished between 1760 and 1850. Whatman's paper was invariably used for many of the quality maps and prints published during this period. His paper is almost always dated, in addition to carrying his name and mark. The maps of John Cary, Edward Mogg and others, were greatly enhanced by the use of this quality paper. A study of water-marks can provide a lifetime's research for anyone so inclined. There are few books on the subject but some titles are included in the bibliography and may be helpful for further study.

I have attempted to reproduce some of the more interesting marks found on maps in the collection. Their detection has not been easy due to the engraved detail of the map often obscuring the mark. This is made even more difficult with maps that carry text on their backs.

The example illustrated (fig.1.) appears on the map of Wales by Lhuyd taken from the Additamentum of the Ortelius Atlas of 1573 and is a plain capital letter 'P' within a shield. The map of England and Wales was also published in the Additamentum, but the mark of the crossed arrows (fig.2) appears on the edition of 1578, as well as on some first editions of Saxton's Atlas.

Mercator's map of the British Isles after Ptolemy published in 1578 carries a fine mark of a crowned double headed Eagle (fig.3) Variations of this mark appear to have been in use before the sixteenth century. Mr. Heawood dates this mark between 1589 and 1595 (The Geographical Journal Vo. LXIII, 1924) which appears to cast doubt on the probability of my copy of Mercator's Ptolemy being a first edition, although the Atlas is dated 1578. Some re-engraving of cartouches appeared in later editions, but the maps in this one are from the first state of the plates. A subsequent edition of the Atlas in 1584 would still predate the first recorded use of this mark by five years. In the Hondius edition published in 1605, the text is in Latin and Greek. As my copy is in Latin, it can only be the original edition of 1578 or that of 1585. Either appears to confirm that this mark was in use before 1589 and illustrates the kind of interesting study that watermarks can provoke.

The miniature map of Britain taken from the rare little Bertius Atlas, carries a small fleur-de-lys or lily mark with what appears to be a scroll beneath (fig 4) although part of the mark is lost at the edge of the paper. A similar lily mark is found on some of the maps in the Ogilby Road Atlas. This very popular mark was in use as early as 1468. There is a very large example on the Tuke map of Holderness issued in 1794 (fig 11). The Mercator issue of Lhuyd's map of Wales carries a most attractive mark with a monogram formed by letters 'F.O.M.' within a decorative shield. Mr. Heawood is of the opinion that this is a German paper, possibly make in Frankfurt, and in use between 1596 and 1613, which ties in with the publication date of this map in 1607. (Fig 5)

Camden's 1637 map of Lancashire carries a small grapes mark (fig.6). This originated in Italy and later spread to France, where it became so well known that a paper size was named after it. Early examples tend to be small and irregular, later ones are larger and less artistic. The 1662 edition of Speed's map of Wiltshire carries a similar mark. I have found no less than five different marks in my 1637 copy of Camden's *Britannia* all displaying various armorials.

Drayton's map of Somerset and Wiltshire issued in 1613 carries a small 'pot' mark (fig.7) also believed to be of French origin. This is a mark found in many different forms on later eighteenth century papers. The Foolscap mark (fig.8) on Blome's Somerset map published in 1673, is a fine example of this popular mark, often found on British made paper from the early seventeenth century. Cromwell is said to have insisted that this watermark should be used in place of paper bearing the Crown or Royal Cypher during the Commonwealth period, but there is little evidence to support this and the mark was frequently used by later European makers.

The 1722 edition of Camden's *Britannia* contains maps by Robert Morden most of which carry a large water mark of a horse within a circle. This is believed to be a mark of Italian origin (fig.9). The mark found on both Bickham's Birds Eye View of Warwickshire published in 1750, and on the Badeslade and Toms map of Middlesex of 1742 was originally a mark used on high quality Dutch paper known as 'Pro Patria' which had been specially developed for use with official documents. It was first made as early as 1683 when the design depicted the Maid of Holland within a ring fence holding a stick with a hat on top. The Dutch Lion is also present, holding a sword in one paw with a bundle of seven arrows in the other.

The arrows are believed to portray the need of the Seven Provinces to protect themselves from outside aggression. By the early 1700's this mark had been altered and looked very similar to the example (fig 10) in use during the mid-eighteenth century. From this date, British paper-makers adopted the design, substituting the Maid of Holland for a seated figure of Britannia!

The fine Whatman watermark (fig 11) is very large, measuring some 8 inches overall. The design incorporates the fleur-de-lys or lily emblem within a shield, with a crown above. The letter 'W' is incorporated at the lower end of the device and the paper is also watermarked 'J. Whatman'. and dated 1794. Whatman appears to have been one of the first British papermakers to actually date paper by means of watermarks. It is perhaps a little ironic that having learned his paper making skills in Holland, Whatman returned to England where he established a mill at Maidstone and for almost a century supplied most of the quality printing paper for the British market, previously supplied by the Dutch.

Map Colouring

Watercolour was used to decorate early maps although some will be found in their original black and white state. If the colour on a map appears to have been printed, it is very unlikely to be antique. Colour printed lithographic maps were introduced towards the end of the nineteenth century and will soon be antiques in their own right. If well applied, the hand colouring on a map adds to its attraction. Poor quality colouring tends to reduce the maps general attractiveness and its worth.

Few early maps published in atlas form were coloured, although as time went on this situation changed. Ortelius first entered the map-making field as a colourist and later achieved world renown as a publisher of atlases. The publication of John Speed's Atlas in the early seventeenth century introduced a new decorative dimension into map-making. Speed adorned his maps with armorial shields of the nobility and gentry. To indicate the correct colours, engravers used either a code letter or shaded the armorials in a certain manner. Seven colours are employed in heraldry; gold and silver, known as metals, and blue, red, black, green and purple, termed tinctures. In heraldic language, gold is known as 'or' and is identified by the initial 'o', or by a stipple or dotted engraved pattern. Silver (argent) is identified by the letter 'a' only. Blue (azure) is letter 'b' or defined by horizontal lines. Red (gules) is indicated by the letter 'g' and has vertical lines. Black (sable) is lettered 's' and combines both horizontal and vertical lines. Green (vert) is letter 'v' and employs diagonal shading running from top left to bottom right. Purple (purpure) carries the letter 'p' with diagonal lines running in the opposite direction, i.e. top right to bottom left.

Most of the colours used to decorate early maps were of vegetable origin quite unlike the mineral based watercolours in use today. Sadly the green usually contained verdigris which can cause serious damage to paper.

Maps removed from an atlas which have hitherto been protected from direct light, will often darken appreciably over any areas coloured green for light appears to accelerate the action of the acid attack. A recent severe example that comes to mind was a Lhuyd map of Wales where a boundary area coloured green simply fell out of the map as if cut by scissors. There are remedies for maps affected by verdigris. The green areas can be treated by a chemical application which neutralizes the action of the acid and the map may be backed or 'laid down' by pasting on a suitable stiff paper. In either case the work requires care and skill and is best undertaken by a professional restorer.

The famous house of Blaeu of Amsterdam distinguished itself with the issue of atlases that were superbly hand-coloured before publication. Of particular interest to collectors of Welsh Blaeu county maps is the fact that on copies carrying the Arms of the Princes of Wales, the colouring was wrongly executed. The entire field of the shield was coloured red and the four lions gold. The correct description of the Arms of Llywelyn, Prince of Wales is quarterly, Or (gold) and Gules (red) four lions passant gardant counter-changed. If your Welsh Blaeu carries this correct colouring, it is unlikely to have been hand-coloured at the time the Atlas was issued, for the Blaeus' never corrected this error.

Care of Maps

The fact that many old maps have survived the test of time is ample proof of the care that went into the paper making process. Antique maps have four principal enemies; heat, damp, insects and careless humans. Frequently, one sees valuable items hanging above open fireplaces and over radiators and this localised heat can be particularly harmful to the paper on which early maps and prints are printed. Excessive heat will cause the paper to dry out and become brittle, resulting in eventual disintegration.

Do not hang maps where they are likely to receive direct sunlight as this is likely to cause fading of the colouring and bleaching of the paper. Unframed items should always be stored flat, never rolled. If it is necessary to send an item through the post, ensure that you use at least a 4" diameter roll, rolling the item round the outside of the tube with a protective covering of tissue and corrugated paper.

Where old maps have been stored under very damp conditions, discolouration will occur and sometimes a fungus growth will develop. This is likely to spread and rotting will follow. If detected in time, cleaning and sizing by a professional restorer will usually prevent further trouble. Most old papers are capable of absorbing appreciable amounts of moisture without damage and a moisture content of 10% is not likely to prove harmful. In general terms, a cooler atmosphere is better than the near tropical temperatures prevailing in some centrally heated homes.

Insect damage is most likely to be caused by woodworm or silver fish. Damage by the former often took place whilst maps were in atlases and instances of woodworm boring right through an atlas are not uncommon. The old plywood backs of pictures that have been framed for some considerable time are often badly affected by woodworm. This material is not recommended for backing maps, hardboard being much more suitable. The picture framer of a century ago used several wide strips of thin wood for this backing, covered with a stiff paper to provide an effective seal. Eventually, the paper breaks along the edges of the joints and a map or a print hanging in a fairly light location, will in time display evidence of the joint lines on the printed surface of the item. If this is allowed to continue, discoloration and disintegration of the paper will result.

Silver fish operate somewhat differently from woodworm. These tiny torpedo-shaped silvery insects are about $\frac{3}{8}$" long and possess a remarkable turn of speed. They eat the surface (and the impression) of your unframed map or print if it is left undisturbed for any length of time. Their favourite meal is the fine top surface of old lithographs, so they can be more of a problem to the collector of old prints. Frequently, they will eat their way along the surface of a map, taking the inked impression with them without penetrating the paper. If you store unframed maps in any quantity, good old-fashioned moth balls will keep them away.

Many discriminating collectors will not permit their unframed maps to be handled by others because of the possible risk of damage by careless handling.

Collectors who are prepared to let friends handle rare and valuable items should stress the need for care.

Small maps should be supported on the open palm or palms of the hands when thumbs should not be in evidence! Holding an old map open like a newspaper with the thumbs uppermost will most certainly damage the margins as old papers bruise and crease very easily. Larger maps are best placed on a piece of stiff card of suitable size, when gentle pressure with either thumb will allow them to be moved without mishap. Handling and inspection should be careful and unhurried, with smoking and beverages kept well out of the way. It is as well to give early warning about any items that are particularly fragile, so that they can be handled with extra care.

I find it a sobering thought that some of the maps in my collection have already passed their four-hundredth birthday thanks to the loving care of previous custodians. The dedicated collector with his interest and concern for conservation, is a vital link in a chain that is helping to ensure their continued enjoyment by future generations.

Presenting your collection

If it is one's intention to start a collection it is first necessary to decide whether to keep the maps in a folio, or frame them to give added pleasure and interest. You may decide to frame the items yourself by locating a supplier who will cut and mitre the moulding at a small extra charge.

Traditionally, maps were framed either in a plain black frame (still known today as map-moulding) or in a black and gilt ornamental moulding termed Hogarth. The most satisfactory method of framing ought to combine the old advantages with modern furnishing requirements. Usually a ¾ or 1 inch width moulding is used together with a gold slip which is fitted beneath the glass and effectively prevents the map touching it. This is an important consideration, especially where central heating is concerned. Condensation forming on the inside of the glass could be transferred to the map, leading to discolouration and damage. This simple precaution will allow air to circulate over the surface of the item permitting it to 'breathe' and is an essential aspect of conservation that is all too often overlooked. Today's picture framer uses the term 'close framed' for an item presented in this way.

If you decide to use a wood moulding, don't spoil the presentation by using one that is too narrow. An ½" width moulding used to frame a Speed map is false economy because the frame will eventually distort, due to the weight of the glass.

A popular and more common alternative before framing is card mounting. This is simply a fairly thick piece of card, or mounting board, with a "cut-out" window into which the map is fitted. It is usual for the window to be cut somewhat larger than the map's border, so that the plate mark remains visible. The map should be attached to the back of the mount by a couple of tabs made from gummed paper, one on each of the corners. Cellotape, masking tape or similar adhesive tapes are unsuitable for this purpose and their use should be discouraged. This alternative method is quite effective in keeping the map free of the glass, but for the purist, the slip is the answer as card window mounts were first introduced as recently as 1900, by a member of the British Museum Print Room Staff.

As mentioned elsewhere, there is often interesting text on the backs of most old maps. To enable this to be read after the item has been framed, it is customary to fit a second piece of glass to the back of the frame instead of the usual backing. Double glazed items are, of course, vulnerable and should be handled with extra care.

Investment Values

The astute collector has long recognised that antique maps represent a first class investment. Good quality antiques of all kinds are now difficult to find and their scarcity is reflected in the increasing prices one has to pay. I hear experienced collectors bemoaning the fact that the

Speed map they bought seven years ago for £20 now costs £250 or more. He will be fortunate indeed who, in ten years time can find one for sale, let alone afford to purchase it.

Antique maps have been greatly underpriced for years and dealers are at last beginning to realise that they have sold stocks, built up during a lifetime's trading, that cannot be replaced. It is of interest to the collector of limited means that the race is not always to the richest. A Speed map purchased two years ago for £150 would certainly sell today for about double that sum. A similar sum expended on Owen and Bowen County maps would have enabled the collector to acquire about thirty of them, worth today, in unframed state, about four times the original investment.

This comparison is interesting because it shows that the growth rate on some lesser maps has outpaced the more expensive ones. The Owen and Bowen, the Moule and the Moll are three types of maps which have been singled out by the wise collector. The county maps of Van den Keere are another good example of miniature maps showing marked appreciation. The growth rate on most 17th and 18th century maps is now between 50 and 100% per annum and likely to rise even more dramatically in the years ahead as supplies become exhausted.

The smaller atlases tended to be in regular use in their day, so it is not surprising that their mortality rate was high. Not so the large tomes of Speed and others, which often sat on the library shelves of the nobility and gentry for a century or more.

The choice available to the new collector is wide, ranging in price from a few pounds to many hundreds. Visit as many dealers as you can, comparing the quality and conditions of their stock. The wise dealer will usually place his professional know-how at the disposal of his regular clientele. Remember that knowledge will always pay better dividends than money. The collector who has done his homework will have a head start on the man with money to spare, but little knowledge.

If you travel, you may find that a Speed of Wiltshire on sale in Glasgow, costs less than a similar one in Salisbury, although this is less likely now than it was a few years ago. Until you are able to trust your own judgment nothing is lost in asking for a certificate of authenticity.

Some eight years ago, the writer purchased a complete Saxton Atlas from a London dealer for £3,500. In order to do this it was necessary to raise a bank loan of £1,000 to complete the purchase. Rather stupidly, a short term arrangement was requested and some months later when the time for re-payment was due, found himself having to sell the Atlas to a

14

collector friend. The Atlas bearing the Duke of Marlborough's book-plate, was recently valued in excess of £30,000.

There are a number of conclusions to be drawn from this inept piece of high finance which may be of value to intending investors. First, always look for quality and rarity in any purchase you make. There can be no finer buy in the field of British cartography than an original map by Christopher Saxton. Secondly, buy the best you can afford but avoid over-reaching yourself. Most people have responsibilities as well as a desire to invest wisely. Thirdly, always buy from reputable sources where the extensive knowledge of the dealer is coupled with his integrity and reputation. Finally, if you are to become a front rank investor, never permit any collecting sentiment to cloud your judgement. By this means, given the necessary initial capital, you are likely to die wealthy, but perhaps without any real idea of what life is all about!

Original Saxton maps (not to be confused with the Camden issues that also bear his name) are now extremely rare and difficult to find. Asking prices range between £1,400 and £2,000 each and are beyond the reach of most of us. On the other hand it is still possible to buy good examples of Lhuyd's maps of Wales or his England and Wales from Ortelius. These two maps are undervalued at present and are the first published maps of the two countries dating from 1573.

Maps by the famous engravers Kip and Hole that first appeared in Camden's *Britannia* in 1607 were once common but are now difficult to find as far as the important counties are concerned. Costing upwards of £60 a piece, they still have a long way to go.

The somewhat later County maps by John Speed are more common than their Saxton counterparts, but again prices have risen steeply in recent years and major counties are costing in excess of £300 each and still rising. Examples of Blaeu and Jansson, possibly the most decorative series of maps ever produced, have been rather slower in the league tables. A few years ago they were very common, due to the large number of atlases printed. They may still be bought for prices of £100 upwards and nice examples will readily double in value over the next few years.

John Ogilby's Road Atlas is now a scarce item and good examples from this work are likely to command prices in excess of £100 each before very long. The Owen and Bowen road-maps are still fairly easy to obtain but county maps from this miniature series are really making ground for the more important counties. Whilst on the subject of miniature maps don't overlook some of the later 18th and 19th century examples. The scarce decorative Perrot series of miniature county maps are still undervalued.

It makes good sense to have ones name placed on the mailing lists of the more important map dealers and auction rooms as well as to keep an eye out for any maps that may be offered through the smaller country rooms not regularly visited by the trade.

There will always be bargains to be found and the experienced collector in the right place at the right time will use his knowledge and judgement to acquire them.

Reproductions and Fakes

All the maps in my collection with two exceptions were purchased from map-dealers in the United Kingdom, a number coming via the important London Salerooms; they are none the worse for that. I have sometimes bought bargains in the trade, but only rarely have antique maps from private sources been offered. The wise collector will keep an eye open for the antique shop that carries the odd map. Make sure it is authentic before you purchase and obtain a certificate to this effect, otherwise you may have no redress in law if you have bought a clever reproduction. Remember that attractive hand-colouring on a map is no proof of age.

There are a number of reproduction maps coming onto the market at the present time that are clearly intended to deceive. The present trend appears to be towards copying the more expensive maps of Saxton and Speed including the World Hemisphere and Americas maps by Speed. The high prices that originals of these maps now command make them an attractive proposition for the forger. An old frame, backed with newspaper displaying a date around 1890 provides no guarantee that the map wasn't framed yesterday.

Clearly the best safeguard when buying expensive originals is the knowledge and integrity of the professional map dealer.

What to Collect

A map collection based on a particular theme is likely to be more interesting and valuable than a haphazard selection. In my own case, I have attempted to bring together a representative collection of maps of the United Kingdom, spanning some four hundred years, including some of the less well-known examples.

For the reader proposing to start collecting on a small annual budget, the maps of the early 1800's have a great deal to commend them. The collection after twelve months could number ten or a dozen maps if bought from the usual trade sources, perhaps more with wise buying from bookshops and the smaller antique and bric-a-brac dealers. The great delight of collecting in this price range is that one can still specialise, be the choice county maps, a particular map-maker, or perhaps maps showing the development of the country's roads, canals, or railway network.

Supply sources of old maps are drying up fast and dealer's discounts have suffered as a result. However bookshops dealing in old books and atlases are worth a call as they sometimes convert damaged books, or "breakers" into mounted individual items. Keen collectors rarely pass on details of their sources to fellow collectors, though by not doing so they probably lose out in the long run.

Research and Reference

The title for this section may sound a little dull and uninteresting and, if after reading it, your observations are confirmed, then perhaps map collecting is not for you. Knowledge of one's subject is essential to success in any field. I am reminded of the old map dealer who said that if he had to make a choice between money or knowledge he would chose the latter, because knowledge could not be bought.

There are a number of ways open to the newcomer that will help him become a discriminating and successful collector. He must read as much about the subject as he can by acquiring suitable reference books.

These are frequently expensive but the resources of the public library services are not! All large libraries have reference sections which may be consulted. They are invariably staffed by well qualified people whose help and advice is readily available. Some of the books mentioned in the booklist will be on their shelves, others can be obtained from regional sources. A good example of a book they should be able to provide not normally found on the shelves of local book sellers is *Book Auction Records*. This annual work catalogues many of the sales in the United

Kingdom of rare books, atlases and maps, together with the names of the individual purchaser's and the prices paid. A useful spin-off from *Auction Records* are the trade advertisements which will enable a list to be compiled of the names and addresses of dealers in old maps.

If one is fortunate to live or work in the London area the city can be your oyster. Here are to be found more book-sellers and map-dealers to the square mile than in any other city in the world. In addition to the larger establishments, many smaller dealers work in tiny premises, in basements and back streets, as well as in the various antique markets.

Armed with a suitable list of names and addresses, one now has the opportunity to visit dealers and inspect their stocks, taking note of the quality, condition and price of the various items they have to offer. One hopes that the advice given earlier about careful handling will be heeded. An experienced dealer can tell at a glance by the way a customer handles his stock whether he is to be trusted with his better quality maps. Initially, it is probably best to make a specific request, say for maps of a particular county when the appropriate folio will be brought for your inspection. After careful examination, place each item face down on the cover of the folio.

After your examination, the dealer will usually close the folio himself and return it to its accustomed place. Unless you are known to the dealer it is not usual to open drawers or take out folios for inspection without first seeking permission.

Your interest in old maps may be stimulated as a result of reading this book but for financial or other reasons you may not choose to become a collector. Many fine examples of rare maps are to be found in libraries and museums throughout Britain, the most important collection being in the Map Library which is a part of the British Library. It is located on the mezzanine floor of the King Edward Building on the north side of the British Museum. It provides its own reader services with an open access reference library and is open from 9.30 a.m. to 4.30 p.m. on weekdays and Saturdays.

For admission to the Map Library and its facilities a Reader's Pass is necessary (form R.D.R.A.8). In certain circumstances a temporary pass can be issued to visitors seeking specific research information.

Each year the Map Library handles a great many requests from all over the world. Postal enquiries must be explicit, giving as much detail on the item as possible, including the dimensions. A photograph can be a positive aid to identification. Often requests are made to the Library for information that is already available from local reference sources, or from a visit to a map specialist. The Library is not able to offer valuations.

Sometimes reference information is available from local historical or similar societies whose members are only too happy to share a common interest. Local library and museum services are often able to refer one to other interested individuals in a particular district. This might lead to a study group being formed with sponsorship from the Local University or perhaps the Workers' Educational Association.

Security and Insurance

Now a word about safeguarding and insuring your collection. Insurers usually require a valuation from an approved authority, although they may be prepared to accept receipted invoices for valuation purposes. The appreciation rate on certain rare items can be in excess of one hundred per cent per annum and old maps are no exception. This high appreciation will quickly outstrip the cover provided by inflation linked household policies. If the value of a collection is in excess of £1,000 it will be necessary to discuss the question of special insurance cover with a broker or insurance company.

The serious collector appreciates the importance of keeping a satisfactory record of his collection. This is simple and inexpensive to introduce. A few packs of plain postcards will provide a suitable basis for a card index, using a separate card for each item. The heading should include the name of the map and the date of issue, if known, followed by the date of purchase, the price paid and the name and address of the supplier, together with details of any security prefix and its whereabouts on the map. The recorded value of each item should be updated annually. The larger map dealers issue regular catalogues which can provide a useful guide to current prices.

The practice of affixing receipts to the back of framed maps is not recommended. Individuals who are not collectors sometimes buy the odd expensive map with an eye to investment. They imagine that leaving the receipt on the back will prevent a loved one giving the item to a charity auction in the event of their untimely death. It may also provide an intruder with evidence that the item is not a reproduction and encourage him to include it in his haul!

The increase in value of many old maps, coupled with the difficulty of identifying them once they have been removed from atlases, has resulted in a frightening increase in the number of thefts from libraries, museums, auction rooms and dealers' stocks. The police advise the photographing of valuable antiques to assist in tracing stolen items. Alas, a Speed map removed from one atlas looks very much like its counterpart taken from another. Many libraries and public bodies are now security-marking their collections.

One of the special pens used is marketed by Volumatic of Coventry. It looks like a normal ballpoint and is available from most security firms at a cost of a few pounds. In use, the pen leaves a visible trace on the paper to show that it is working, which quickly disappears. Thereafter, the marking can only be detected by means of ultra-violet scanning equipment of the kind used by the police. My own collection is marked in this way with a monogram on the face of the map itself, rather than in the margin, which can be cut off. The suppliers claim that there is no risk to the map by marking it in this manner. I was recently interested to learn from a Danish collector that the police in his country will only seriously investigate the theft of maps that have been security marked because they consider the chance of recovering unmarked items so difficult as to be almost impossible.

Perhaps the day is not too far distant when dealers in the map trade will realise the very real need to security mark expensive items. Maps could be marked with a prefix letter that identifies the firm, followed by a stock number. A record card supplied to the purchaser would give details of the marking and essential information as to ownership would be updated each time the map changed hands.

Collectors and dealers buy from each other or from private individuals. Both need to be especially careful when buying from unknown third parties. I know several dealers and private collectors who have had cause to regret certain good buys that later turned into 'goodbyes' because they had unwittingly bought stolen goods! If you are the least doubtful about an intended purchase, particularly if the price appears to be on the low side, or if cash is insisted upon 'because of the Tax man' you would be well advised not to buy. When dealing with strangers always ask the seller to sign a simple indemnity stating that the goods in question are his own unencumbered property and that he or she agrees to indemnify you against any claims arising out of the purchase by you. This should be signed by the seller and witnessed by a third party (not his wife) whose address, together with the date of the transaction, should be included. This precaution will ensure that you are not charged with 'receiving' at some later date should your purchase turn out to have been previously stolen.

Sometimes, a collector's interest is not shared by the other partner, but a collection can be of great financial benefit to a surviving spouse should the collector die. It is, therefore, necessary to make provisions, either in a Will or with some other written instruction to enable the collection to realise its true value if it should be sold. One satisfactory means of disposal is via the important London auction rooms. Antique maps are a rather specialised branch of collecting and are not likely to achieve realistic prices if offered to local antique dealers.

Much of the remainder of the book is taken up with details on some of the many and varied maps of Britain that have been published, together with indications of current market prices (see insert) and other information likely to be of help to the newcomer to this absorbing pastime.

The rating number set against each map illustrated is an attempt to indicate the degree of difficulty likely to be experienced in obtaining a similar copy, viz:-

1	=	Rare
2	=	Scarce
3	=	Very difficult
4	=	Difficult
5	=	Easier to obtain

The dimensions given are in inches and millimetres measured to the outside of the printed border, with the height quoted first.

Important Dates in Map-Making

150 A.D. Marinus of Tyre in first half of second century A.D. was the first to calculate latitude and longtitude of individual place in degrees instead of linear distances. The work of Marinus was completed and perfected by Claudius Ptolemy, who compiled data for a map of the then known world using simple conical projection.

1466 Donnus Nicolas Germanus, a German who worked in Florence, redrew the Ptolemy Atlas on a new trapeziod projection introducing figures for latitude and longitude.
(History of Cartography—R. A. Skelton, P. 78)

1493	Pope Alexander IV settled disputes between Spain and Portugal by drawing a meridian 100 leagues from the Azores. All lands to the west of this meridian were assigned to Spain and all lands to the east to Portugal.
1667	Acadamie Royale met to establish the meridian of Paris as the standard meridian of longitude for all nations.
1761	John Harrison perfected the chronometer thus enabling longitude to be determined.
1884	International agreement established the meridian of Greenwich as 0° Longitude

The Maps

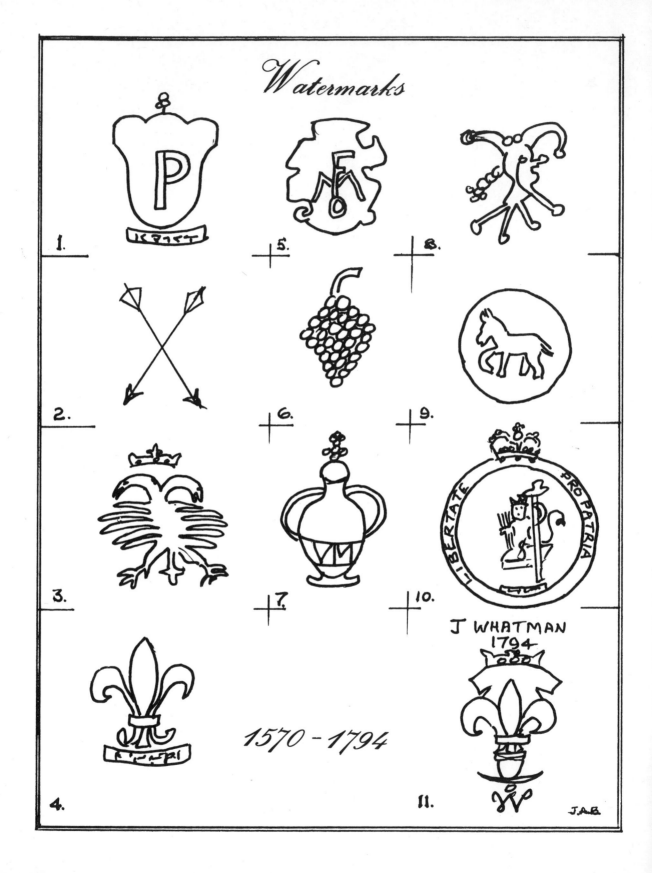

Watermarks

1.

2.

3.

4.

5.

6.

7.

8.

9.

10.

J WHATMAN
1794

11.

1570 - 1794

J.A.B

Humphrey Lhuyd, 1527-1568

Maps Nos. 1 & 2

In 1573, Abraham Ortelius published an Additamentum or supplement to his famous world Atlas *Theatrum Orbis Terrarum* first published in 1570. It contained two maps taken from manuscripts sent to him by Humphrey Lhuyd of Denbigh. Lhuyd, born at Denbigh in 1527 is known to have completed his studies at Oxford in 1551 where he received a Master of Arts degree. He later became an author and topographical writer and was for a number of years personal physician to Lord Arundel. Doubtless the maps he prepared were intended to illustrate his writings but it was through the good offices of Sir Richard Clough, a merchant from Denbigh, that contact with Ortelius was made which lead to the publication of these two maps.

One is a well detailed map of England and Wales, bearing a date of 1573 which appeared in subsequent editions of the atlas until replaced in the early seventeenth century with a map of the British Isles by Johan Baptist Vrints. The other is Lhuyd's general map of Wales which also made its first appearance in the Additamentum of 1573 and continued to be included in the Atlas until 1612, without any major alterations to the layout of the printing plate.

These two maps were the first of England and Wales to be published. The one of England and Wales is finely engraved with elegant swash lettering used to name the various seas on which are depicted men o' war and other sailing vessels of the period. A large oval ornamental cartouche carries the title of the map, together with Lhuyd's name printed in Latin. Two nude maidens as Supporters, hold a device bearing the Royal Arms of the Tudors, erroneously engraved in reverse. The cartouche is dated 1573, as were later issues making them difficult to date. The sea is stippled and about 1595 additional stippling was introduced, and the earlier 'label' effect surrounding the lettering was lost. This information can be helpful in determining whether a particular map was published before, or after, 1595. (See Dr. North's Humphrey Lhuyd's Maps of England and Wales).

A detailed study of the map will reveal the use of the circle as a symbol to depict settlements. This is used in conjunction with tiny buildings drawn in elevation, to denote churches, castles, or both. Mountains, hills, woodland and forest receive similar picturesque treatment. Though rivers abound, there are no roads and few counties are named.

No. 1   Humphrey Lhuyd map of England & Wales, Ortelius, 1573 (1579)

The map of Wales has a cartouche in the upper left hand corner with the title and Lhuyd's name in Latin within an elaborately bordered panel decorated with oak leaves and acorns. The sea is stippled in a similar manner to the previous map and shows a three masted sailing ship in Cardigan Bay and a sea monster, possibly a whale, surfacing off Fishguard. The scale of miles, together with a pair of open dividers, is located in the lower left hand corner of the map. There is also a table giving regional information in English, Welsh and Latin.

The map is very inaccurate as far as the south coast of Wales is concerned and bears interesting comparison with Saxton's map of Glamorganshire published some five years later. Saxton's delineation of the Gower peninsular compares favourably with modern examples, but his coastline from Aberavon around to Cardiff is much too angular. It was nevertheless religiously copied by other map publishers including Camden, Speed and Blaeu.

Later, this map received similar treatment to the stippling around the lettering in the sea as did the one of England and Wales. The re-engraving is thought to have taken place about 1580, but I have seen two German examples of 1580 with and without this additional stippling. Individual copies of the map are not easy to date after 1588, when subsequent issues carried the same folio number (13) on the back. (See table).

Folio editions of the Theatrum of Ortelius containing
Lhuyd's Map of Wales.
States 1 and 2

	Edition	Text	Folio/ Map No.	Edition	Text	Folio/ Map No.
1st state	1573	Latin Additamentum	6C	1592	Latin	13
		German „	6C			
	1573	Latin	9	1595	Latin	13
	1573	German	9	1598	Dutch	13
	1574	Latin	9	1598	French	13
	1575	Latin	9	1601	Latin	13
	1578	French	9	1602	Spanish	13
	1579	Latin	11	1602	German	13
2nd state	1580	German	11	1603	Latin	13
	1581	French	11	1606	English	13
	1584	Latin	12	1608	Italian	13
	1507	French	12	1600	Latin	13
	1588	Spanish	12	1612	Latin	13
	1591	Latin	13	1612	Spanish	13

N.B. From 1588 to 1612 individual maps are difficult to date exactly. All were from the second state of the plate, but many editions in the same language bear the same folio number. For example, there were seven Latin editions all bearing the folio No. 13.

ANGLIÆ PARS olim LHOEGR appellata

Aliqua Regionum huius tractus finitima, prout Latinè, Britannicè &c, Anglicè criennam appellantur.

Cambria. L.
Cambry. B.
Wales. A.

Venedotia. L.
Guynedhia. B.
Northwales. A.

Demetia. L.
Dyfet. B.
Wefthwales. A.

Ceretica. L.
Ceredigion. B.
Cardigan. A.

Poufia. L.
Powys. B.

Debenbart. B.
Sutwales. A.

Mona infula. L.
Anglesey. A.
Mon. B.

CAMBRI
AE TYPVS
Auctore
HVMFRE
DO LHV:
YDO
Denbigienfe Cam:
brobritano

VERGIVIVM SIVE HIBERNICVM MARE
MOR WERIDH, Britannis,
THE YRISHE OCEANE, Anglis.

HI:
BER:
NIAE
PARS.

Cum Privilegio.

Scala Milia:
rium Anglicorum.

No. 2   Humphrey Lhuyd map of Wales, Ortelius 1573

A new version of the map appeared in the Mercator-Hondius Atlas from 1607 (until 1633) printed from a somewhat smaller plate engraved by Pieter Van den Keere. The ornamental strapwork cartouche carries the engraver's name in Latin 'Petrus Kaerius' which readily identifies it. This plate was re-engraved for the Jansson Atlas of 1636-1642 when a large oval ornamental cartouche was introduced in the top left hand corner with two baskets of fruit suspended on garlands.

The third and final state of the map published from 1647 onwards, has a smaller oval cartouche, now moved to the top right hand corner with two cherubs as Supporters and the stippling of the sea is omitted.

The original manuscripts for these maps were sent to Ortelius in 1568, the year of Lhuyd's death, but it is likely that their compilation took place at least five years previously. Despite the primitive nature of surveying in the mid-sixteenth century, the general outline of the two countries is surprisingly accurate although the coastal region of south west England lies in a westerly rather than a south-westerly direction.

Tragically, Humphrey Lhuyd died at the early age of forty-one, five years before his maps were published. Nevertheless, his significant contribution to British cartography continues to live on in the maps he so painstakingly prepared.

England and Wales size $14\frac{7}{8}$ inches $\times$ $18\frac{3}{8}$ inches   Rating 2
(378mm $\times$ 467mm)

Wales Ortelius $14\frac{5}{8}$ inches $\times$ $19\frac{7}{8}$ inches   Rating 2
(373mm $\times$ 505mm)

Wales Mercator-J $13\frac{1}{2}$ inches $\times$ $19\frac{1}{4}$ inches   Rating 3
(344mm $\times$ 489mm)

Gerard Mercator, 1512-1594

In 1578 Godefridus Kempen of Cologne published a new edition of Ptolemy's Geography which contained twenty-eight copper plate maps of the world, including the one of the British Isles illustrated. This Atlas was the work of Gerard Mercator, perhaps best remembered for the famous Projection which bears his name. Despite its outdated geographical content, the Atlas was popular with scholars as well as those seeking an example of the work of this now eminent map-maker. He was then sixty-four years of age.

Mercator was born at Rupelmonde, near Antwerp in the year 1512, where his father was a local shoemaker. A wealthy relative impressed with Mercator's youthful ability for things scientific, paid for his education, including studies at the University of Louvain. He subsequently established himself in business as a maker of scientific instruments. His fame as a surveyor and cartographer became well known and he began to revise maps in the light of new information, some of which was provided by the mariners and merchants who were customers for his instruments. In 1564 he prepared a fine large scale map of the British Isles, but his greatest achievement was a world Atlas that was to rival the one by his friend Ortelius, and which was published in 1595, the year following Mercator's death.

The example illustrated is particularly interesting because of the error as far as Scotland is concerned, which is depicted lying in an easterly, rather than a northerly direction. The fine ornamental cartouche provides an example of Mercator's engraving skill. The sea is stippled and decoration includes a sea monster near the west coast of Ireland and fishermen working a seine net off the Thames Estuary. Settlement signs follow the now established pattern and place names are in Latin, the classical language of the time.

The Atlas was re-issued many times between 1578 and 1704, the date of the final issue. Some later alterations were made to the decorative features (see Investing in Maps, Roger Bayton-Williams, page 24) but not to the maps themselves. Contrary to popular belief, copper not wood, was used for plate-making in early atlases, although wood blocks were used towards the end of the fifteenth century, and later during the important Munster period.

Size: 13 inches × 15½ inches   Rating 1
    (330mm × 394mm)

OCEANVS

DEVCALEDONIVS OCEANVS

HYPER BOREVS

OCEANVS

GERMANICVS OCEANVS

Germania III Pars

Galliæ pars

BRI

HIB ernicus

OCCeanus

OCEANVS OCCIDENTALIS

VERGINIVS OCEANVS

Britan nicus OCEANVS

No. 3   Claudius Ptolemy map of the British Isles, Mercator, 1578

Christopher Saxton, c. 1542-1610

Our earliest printed county maps of England and Wales are found in an Atlas prepared by a Yorkshireman, Christopher Saxton and published exactly four hundred years ago in 1579.

There appears to be doubt as to the year of Saxton's birth, thought to be about the year 1542, at Dunningley near Wakefield, in Yorkshire. He was a surveyor by profession although it is doubtful whether he would have found scope for his talents outside a monastic house had he been born a little earlier.

Before the Reformation, the Church had been the principal land-owner in England and Wales and the monks had undertaken surveys and compiled careful and detailed recordings of their holdings. With the coming of the Reformation and subsequent dissolution of the monasteries, valuable records were lost or destroyed. Church property was sold to a new land-owning class at pains to establish title to its new estates as quickly as possible. The nature of Saxton's work involved travelling to various parts of the country and considerable personal contact with landowners, one of whom was Thomas Seckford, a Suffolk nobleman and a Master of Requests to Queen Elizabeth.

Whether the idea for the Atlas was Saxton's or Seckford's is not clear, but the proposal met with the Queen's approval and Saxton commenced his survey, believed to have taken about six years. As the various county surveys were completed the maps were engraved on copper plates by a team of English and Flemish engravers. There seems little doubt that individual maps were on sale before the Atlas was bound and published in 1579, the first national atlas of its kind to be published in any country.

The map of Glamorganshire illustrated carries the inked number 29, in an old hand in the top left and right hand margins and was printed off-centre, presumably to ensure that the centre fold did not pass through the rather splendid sailing ship.

All the maps in the Atlas carries the Royal Arms of Elizabeth and also those of Thomas Seckford. The supporters for the Royal Arms are the Lion and the Dragon rampant. The Dragon was replaced by the Scottish Unicorn when James 1st became King.

Saxton's maps are finely engraved with two distinct lettering styles for place names, capital letters being used for the larger towns and cities, script for the remainder. The sea is dotted or stippled; there

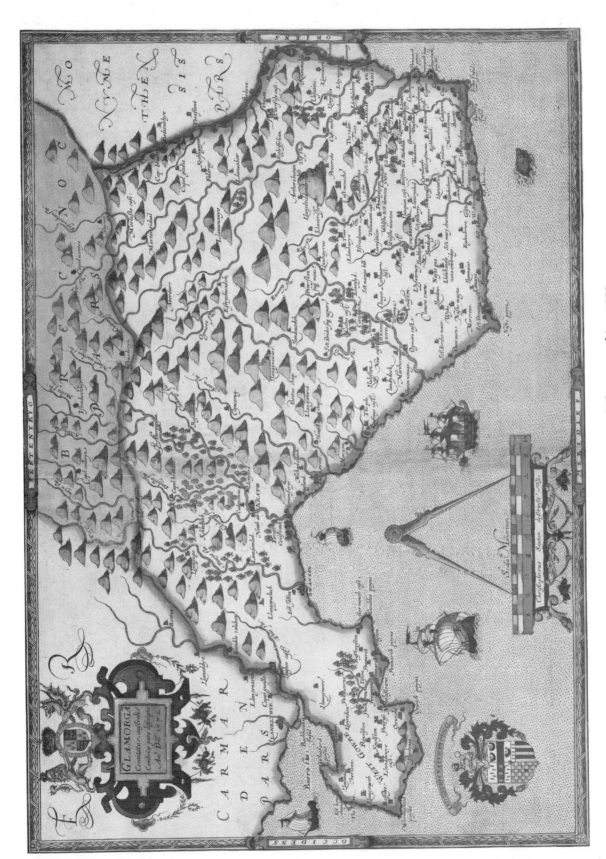

No. 4   Christopher Saxton map of Glamorganshire, 1578

are four sailing vessels and also a sea monster surfacing off 'Barrye': A large pair of dividers surmounts the scale. The hilly regions on the map are depicted by a series of 'molehills' and the parks are bounded by railed fencing. No hundreds are detailed, although both roads and hundreds appear on later issues of the Atlas by Phillip Lea.

There were many printings from the original plates by different publishers from the original edition of 1579 until those by Dicey & Company in 1770.

An edition by William Web dated 1642, published in 1645, with the Arms of Elizabeth replaced by those of Charles 1st is sometimes known as the Civil War Issue and is regarded by many collectors as more of a rarity than the first issue. Phillip Lea published an edition with much altered plates about 1690 in which hundreds, roads and town plans were added, the latter an innovation borrowed from Speed. These copies usually carry contemporary colour to the hundreds only, and even cartouches are left uncoloured. Further issues were published by George Willdey around 1720, by Thomas Jefferys in 1749 and a pale and much worn final issue by Dicey in 1770 from plates nearly two hundred years old!

Size: 13 inches × 19 inches   Rating 1
     (330mm × 482mm)

To the R<small>IGHT</small> H<small>ONOURABLE</small>
JAMES, Earl of C<small>AERNARVAN</small>,
Viſcount *WILTON*, and Baron *CHANDOIS*,

Theſe P L A T E S, containing the direct Roads from *London* throughout *England* and *Wales*, are moſt humbly inſcribed by

His L<small>ORDSHIP</small>'s

Moſt Obedient Servant,

JOHN SENEX.

Petrus Bertius, 1565-1629

Miniature maps are now enjoying something of a collecting vogue perhaps because they provide the purchaser with an opportunity to acquire an example of the work of an early map-maker at a much lower price than is demanded for a conventional example.

This Flemish cartographer and publisher issued a number of interesting works between 1600 and his death in 1629 and served for a time as official Cosmographer to Louis XIII. His best known work was an atlas based on a previous one called *Caert-thresoor* published by Barent Langenes in 1598. The first edition of this Bertius Atlas appeared in 1600 and was followed by a further edition in 1602. Four maps of Britain were included in these early miniature atlases, namely Anglia, Cambria, Scotia and Hibernia. Hondius the Younger enlarged the Atlas by providing a further sixteen maps of Britain in an edition he published in 1616, based on maps from the Mercator-Hondius Atlas. Two further editions were published in 1618 with text in Latin and French. The same plates were later used by Blaeu for his *Abridgement of Camden's Britannia* in 1639.

The example illustrated of Magna Britannia did not appear until the edition of 1616. It is engraved with Britain lying on its side (with west to the top) a practice first introduced by Munster. The title appears in an attractive cartouche in the lower right hand corner and apart from the scale in the upper right hand corner there are no embellishements, although graduations of longitude and latitude appear in the border. The reader will recollect that the use of Greenwich as the meridian for 0° longitude was not established until 1884.

Bertius used the Lhuyd representation of Wales for his map of Cambria but our example of Britain is more accurate than either Lhuyd or Speed; Speed's map presenting something of a top-heavy appearance as far as Scotland is concerned.

These Bertius examples are rare and difficult to find.

Size $3\frac{7}{8}$ inches × $5\frac{3}{8}$ inches   Rating 1
(95mm × 136mm)

No. 5   Petrus Bertius map of Great Britain, 1600 (1616)

William Smith, 1550-1618

Little appears to be known about this Elizabethan cartographer herald (Rouge Dragon) except that he was a contemporary of Saxton and Norden and spent nine years in Germany living in the city of Nurenburg. Dr. Skelton was of the opinion that it was Smith who first drew Norden's attention to the German practice of including a Table of Conventional Signs as well as the grid marking of maps; both practices that were subsequently adopted by Norden for his county maps.

Smith's work was confined to twelve county maps which were based on those of Saxton and Norden, formerly known as the Anonymous series. Roads were also included, together with additional place names.

His map of Surrey is finely engraved and believed to be the work of Jodocus Hondius who prepared many of the plates for Speed's Atlas. The County title in Latin appears within a decorative panel in the upper left hand corner. A similar panel in the right hand corner details the hundreds. In the lower left hand, the scale of miles is surmounted by a pair of open dividers and is balanced by the table of conventional signs in the right hand corner, with text in Latin and English. Swash lettering is used for the names of the surrounding counties with Berkshire misnamed Bedfordshire. The map is very similar in appearance to Norden's map of Surrey in the Map Library of the British Museum except that Norden included the Royal Arms in a central position on his example.

This map carries the imprint of Peter Stent and John Overton. Stent published the map as a single item from about 1643 until his death from the Plague in 1665, when ownership of the plate passed to Overton who included it in his Atlas from 1671. The original issues by Stent are extremely rare and copies from the Overton Atlas are also difficult to find.

It is perhaps interesting that Smith and Norden included roads on their maps prepared in the late Sixteenth century, yet this practice was not adopted by other British map-makers until the publication of Robert Morden's County Atlas in 1695.

Size: $14\frac{3}{4}$ inches × $18\frac{3}{4}$ inches   Rating 1
    (375mm × 477mm)

No. 6   William Smith map of Surrey, 1600 (1670)

William Camden, 1551-1623

(with maps by William Kip and William Hole)

The first work to contain a set of County Maps of England and Wales with each county engraved on a separate sheet, was the 1607 edition of William Camden's *Britannia*, printed in Latin.

Camden was a contemporary of Christopher Saxton and an antiquary and scholar. He was educated at St. Paul's School and Magdalen College, Oxford, where he later endowed a Chair of History. He became headmaster of Westminster School and many of his writings were undertaken during school vacations.

His famous classical work *Britannia* was first published in 1586 and provided a history of Britain from pre-Roman times. It was not until the edition of 1607, (the last one published in his lifetime) that Camden included maps of the English and Welsh counties together with maps of Ireland and Scotland. They were prepared by two famous engravers of the day, William Kip and William Hole, based on those of Saxton and Norden.

In the 1607 edition text in Latin appears on the back of the maps and as the paper on which they are printed is rather thin, the lettering sometimes shows through on the face of the map, spoiling the general effect. Two subsequent editions were printed in 1610 and 1637 with plain backs. Plate numbers were added to many of the maps for the 1637 edition. The maps were not issued again after that date.

It is only recently that the merit of those particular maps has found favour with collectors, notwithstanding the fact that they were Elizabethan in origin and pre-date the better known and more common Speed Atlas by several years. They are sometimes confused with the larger and more elaborate Saxton maps, whose name most of them carry, indicating that they owe their origin to the previous work of this cartographer.

The map illustrated was engraved by William Hole and twenty-one of the maps in the Atlas bear his name, the remainder being attributed to William Kip.

Lancashire is one of the most decorative in the Camden series, it is also one of the most expensive and good examples are difficult to find.

The county title in Latin, is contained within an elaborate cartouche in the upper right hand corner of the map. Two children holding olive branches act as Supporters and the positioning of their bodies suggests

No. 7   William Camden map of Lancashire, 1607 (1637)

41

that the engraver met with some anatomical difficulty! The sea is stippled and the scale is superimposed upon it in the lower left hand corner. Open dividers span the scale. Above, is a finely engraved sixteen point compass rose. Place names are in English but names of the surrounding counties are in Latin. There are 'credits' to Saxton and Hole, hence the term Saxton-Hole or Saxton-Kip, often used to describe maps from this work.

Until a few years ago these maps were fairly cheap, presumably because the work enjoyed a wide circulation. Recently, the more popular counties have become scarce and prices have risen steeply. The apparent historical merit of Camden's writings was recognised by a number of important map-makers, including Speed and his text continued in use for something like two hundred years.

Size: $11\frac{1}{2}$ inches × $12\frac{1}{2}$ inches   Rating 3
      (293mm × 317mm)

John Speed, 1552-1629

John Speed was born at Farndon in Cheshire in 1552 and spent the early years of his working life as a tailor, his father's trade. The family appear to have been fairly prosperous and at 28 years of age he was admitted to the Freedom of the Merchant Tailor's Company. His great interests in life were cartography, writing and the study of history. He found a patron in Sir Fulke Greville " . . . which set him free from manual employment and enabled him to pursue his studies, to which he was strongly inclined by the bent of his genius . . . "

The name of Speed is probably the best known of British map-makers and early copies of his maps are now in great demand. The maps he produced were mainly copied from those of Saxton and Norden and were originally intended to illustrate his History of Great Britain. The text on the back of each relates to the special features of the county, based on the earlier researches of Camden.

Two new features were included on Speed's maps; parish hundreds being indicated by dotted lines and inset plans of the County Town and other important towns. These Speed claimed to have personally surveyed, as indicated by the wording "The Scale of Pases" which appears below the plan. The boundary divisions of the hundreds did not appear on his maps of Carnarvon, Denbigh and Flint because the authorities concerned refused to provide the information.

The contract for engraving the copper plates, from which the maps were printed, was placed with Jodocus Hondius, who spent some time working in London where he married the sister of Pieter Van den Keere before returning to Amsterdam, to take over Mercator's business in 1604.

It seems likely that most of the plates for the Atlas were engraved in Amsterdam, although there is still speculation whether the first edition of the Atlas was printed in London or Amsterdam. However, credit for the first national Atlas of the British Isles rests firmly on the shoulders of John Speed.

On this map of Wiltshire which was re-issued by 'Roger Rea the Elder and Younger at the Golden Crosse in Cornhill against the Exchange,' in 1662, there appears in the upper left hand corner an inset town plan of the city of Salisbury. The county title 'Wilshire' is placed within a small rectangular panel attached to the plan. The map is flanked by two panels containing fourteen armorials representing 'The Armes of the

No. 8   John Speed map of Wiltshire, 1611 (1662)

Earles of Wilshyre & Salesburye'. In the top right hand corner is a view of Stonehenge surrounded by "A Trenche" and beneath it an ornamental panel containing an account of the origins of Stonehenge with the reference "Constanc king of britanie buryed at stonheg Anno 546". Beneath is a large compass rose resting on a rectangular panel carrying the scale of English miles.

The map has an attractive chainlink border but there is a pre-atlas state where the border carries graduations in latitude and longitude. Due west of Salisbury is the village of 'South Burcomb' and on the opposite side of the river appears the fictitious Wiltshire village of 'Quare' in place of North Burcombe! Mr. Bayton-Williams provides an interesting account of the error on page 9 of his book 'Investing in Maps' It appears that Saxton marked the village without naming it. Speed later used Saxton's map for reference and intending to query the place name, marked the map accordingly. This was overlooked and his notation was engraved on the new Speed map! The error was perpetuated by other map-makers until corrected by Bowen nearly a century and a half later.

Subsequent editions continued to be published for the next one hundred and sixty years. They carry the Sudbury and Humble imprint in 1614, 1616 (Latin text) and 1627. William Humble's imprint in 1646, Roger Rea's in 1662 (some with plain backs), Bassett & Chiswell's in 1676 (the most common edition), Overton's in 1713 and 1743 (plain backed) and finally Dicey's in 1770 (plain backed).

In a comment on the portrait of John Speed engraved by Salomon Savery and published in 1631 the Rev. Granger records that "he died on the 28th July, 1629, having had twelve sons and six daughters by one wife".

Size: 15 inches × 19⅞ inches   Rating 3
       (380mm × 504mm)

Michael Drayton, 1563-1631

Michael Drayton was born at Hertshill, Atherstone, Warwickshire, in 1563, the son of a local butcher. He entered the service of Sir Henry Goodere of Powlesworth, as a Page, who was largely responsible for his education and the encouragement of his literary ability. He enjoyed a considerable reputation as a poet during the reigns of Queen Elizabeth and James 1st, but is best remembered by collectors of early maps for his *Poly-Olbion or a Chorographical description of Tracts, Rivers, Mountains, Forest and other Parts of this renowned Isle of Great Britain*. This was a book of verse about the countryside of England and Wales, illustrated by a series of curious little regional maps from the graver of William Hole, similar in size and appearance to the ones provided by Hole for *Camden's "Britannia"*.

The work was first published in 1612 and contained eighteen maps, the one illustrated depicting part of Somerset and Wiltshire. All the maps are without titles, plate numbers or scale, but the rivers and outstanding landmarks are enhanced by nude female bathers in the rivers and shepherds and shepherdesses on the hilltops.

The maps are of little geographical value, but are unusual, amusing and of considerable decorative merit. They also provide an interesting insight into the dress, and undress, of that period! Hole's treatment of the sea is interesting. He introduced his own variation of tiny waves compared with the stipple (dots) often used by other engravers and quite different from the effect produced by Hondius on the Speed maps.

The book's contents remained unchanged for a subsequent edition published in 1613, although numbers were added. For the final edition published in 1622, ten new maps were added, together with twelve additional verses. The numbers on the maps are not plate numbers but relate to the page of text which follows the map.

No information is available on the number of copies made for the three editions mentioned, but certainly the book was not printed again after 1622. It is unlikely that each edition ran to more than a few hundred copies. It is known that Drayton had difficulty in finding a publisher and that the work did not enjoy any great popularity. These factors result in the complete work being regarded as a rarity and the price of individual maps is likely to be high. There are some clever reproductions in circulation but these are unlikely to trap the experienced collector. The engraving is greyish, rather than black in ap-

No. 9   Michael Drayton map of Somerset/Wiltshire, 1612 (1613)

pearance, and the maps are usually laid down, i.e. stuck to a thin card backing.

Drayton died at the age of 68, in 1631 and was buried in Westminster Cathedral, where a statue was erected by the Countess of Dorset to the memory of " . . . this modest and amiable man".

Size: $9\frac{7}{8}$ inches × $13\frac{1}{8}$ inches   Rating 2

(252mm × 335mm)

Pieter Van den Keere, c. 1571-1646

(Petrus Kaerius)

This highly skilled and prolific Dutch engraver appears to have worked both in Holland and Britain. As mentioned previously, his sister married Jodocus Hondius whilst they were living in London before Hondius returned to Holland to take over Mercator's establishment.

Keere engraved a great many map plates for various publishers including the Lhuyd map of Wales for Mercator's Atlas. His early work included a set of miniature map plates based mainly on Saxton and engraved from 1599 onwards. Additional maps on Scotland and Ireland were also included. Had this series of maps been published in atlas form at that time, Keere would have been the first man to complete an atlas of the British Isles. Each carries the name of the particular county in Latin and some have plain backs. These maps were first printed in Holland and are rare.

The plates were later used and re-issued in Atlas form by Joan Blaeu in 1617, when page numbers were added together with Latin text on the back of the maps. George Humble handled the sale of the Atlas in Britain, later acquiring the plates from Blaeu. He reprinted them, again in atlas form to coincide with his issue of the editions of the Speed Atlas in 1627, 1632 and 1646. Humble claimed that they were " . . . from a farr Larger Volume/Done by John Speed/ . . . " It is clear from the above account that many of the maps, and certainly those of the Welsh counties, were engraved before the first issue of the Speed Atlas; the astute Humble using the popularity of Speed to assist the sales of his "miniature Speed".

Humble had the plates re-worked whilst they were in his ownership, converting the Latin county titles into English. Text in English also appeared on the back of the maps and each was given a plate number in the lower right hand corner.

This map of the county of Southampton-shire (Hampshire) appeared in the 1646 edition of the Atlas published by William Humble, by which time some of the printing plates were showing signs of wear. Usually, lightly engraved areas, are the first to show deterioration as with this example where some engraving in the sea is taking on an indistinct and broken appearance. Both map and county title 'Southamptonshire' are copied from Saxton's earlier map. Norden's map in 1580 called the county 'Hamshire' and Speed used the spelling 'Hantshire'.

Copies of any of the counties from either the earlier Keere issues or

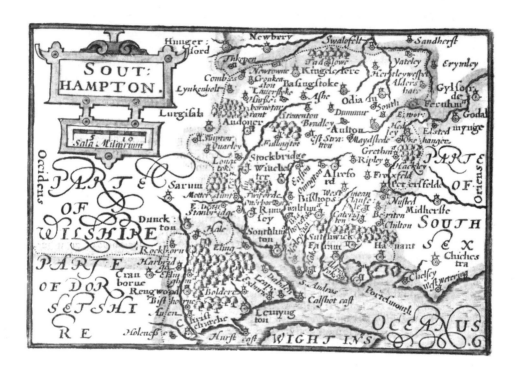

No. 10   Pieter Van den Keere map of Southampton (Hampshire), 1617 (1646)

the Blaeu/Humble editions are well worth including in a collection. A map from the pre-atlas issue, i.e. before 1617, would be a great find. Later publishers of the Speed Atlas continued to produce this miniature Atlas, including the Rea edition in 1662/66 and Basset and Chiswell's in 1676.

Size: $3\frac{3}{8}$ inches × $4\frac{7}{8}$ inches   Rating 3
    (84mm × 121mm)

John Bill, c. 1570-1630

(Camden Abridged)   Map No. 11

This rare little Atlas entitled *The Abridgement of Camden's Britannia* was published by John Bill, a London bookseller in 1626, four years before he died. As the title indicates the maps were based on those of Camden, although Camden's Wiltshire was engraved with east to the top of the map. The maps are interesting because they were the first British county series to carry, in the left hand and lower margins only, a reference to latitude and longitude. Little appears to be known about John Bill although the late Dr. Skelton records that he was in business in Aldergate Street and Blackfriars and shared the office of King's Printer from 1617-30. He also published the *English Ortelius* in association with John Norton in 1606.

The map of Wiltshire has early outline colouring following the county boundaries and the map displays three different copperplate lettering styles. There is little difference in size or appearance between this map and the previous one by Pieter Van den Keere although the engraving lacks the quality of the Keere maps.

The edition of 1626 was the only one to be issued and although there is no information on the size of the edition, it is unlikely to have been more than a few hundred copies. I have only seen half a dozen maps from the atlas in my years as a collector and regard it as the most rare of all our county atlases. In common with other miniature atlases, it doubtless met with a high mortality rate. However, it is worth keeping an eye out for this particular map as there may be fringe dealer's in the trade who might mistake it for a Keere.

Size: $3\frac{1}{8}$ inches $\times$ $4\frac{1}{2}$ inches   Rating 1
       (79mm $\times$ 125mm)

No. 11   John Bill map of Wiltshire, 1626

Jacob Van Langeren Jenner, c.1643

This rare little map, together with its distance table, first appeared in an edition of *A Direction for the English Traveller* published by Thomas Jenner in 1643. Little is known about the engraver Van Langeren, who originally executed the series of thumb-nail maps and distance tables which first appeared in an earlier work, published by Matthew Simmons in 1635.

When Simmons produced his first edition of the Atlas in 1635, it would seem that he used the idea of the distance tables introduced by John Norden in 1625. Norden, a contemporary of Christopher Saxton, was the first British cartographer to include roads on maps. The introduction of distance tables contained in his 'intended guyde for English travailers' was an important step forward, detailing for the first time the distance between towns. However, map publishers for the most part, continued to issue maps for the next one hundred years without showing the roads.

Simmons issued two further editions of the work in 1636, but it was not until after his death, and the edition of 1643 when Jenner had acquired the plates, that the map of Wales was included. This map was one of four larger folding plates included in a new edition. Although the paper is fairly strong, usage and its folding nature has left my own copy in a somewhat delicate state.

Jenner also issued two editions, both in 1668. After his death in 1673 the plates passed to John Garrett who printed an issue in 1677 and a final one about 1680.

Now a word about Thomas Jenner—he was in business as a print-seller at the White Bear in London's Cornhill from 1623 until his death in 1673. He appears to have been a Puritan and staunch supporter of the Parliamentary cause. His Quartermaster's Map engraved by Wenceslaus Hollar and published in 1644 was used by both sides. Hollar for his part, appears to have supported the Royalist cause and was taken prisoner at the seige of Basing House.

Bearing in mind that the earlier editions of the work published by Simmons do not contain this particular map, copies are difficult to find, because the mortality rate on folding maps is high.

Size: $8\frac{7}{8}$ inches $\times$ $8\frac{1}{4}$ inches   Rating 2
    (223mm $\times$ 210mm)

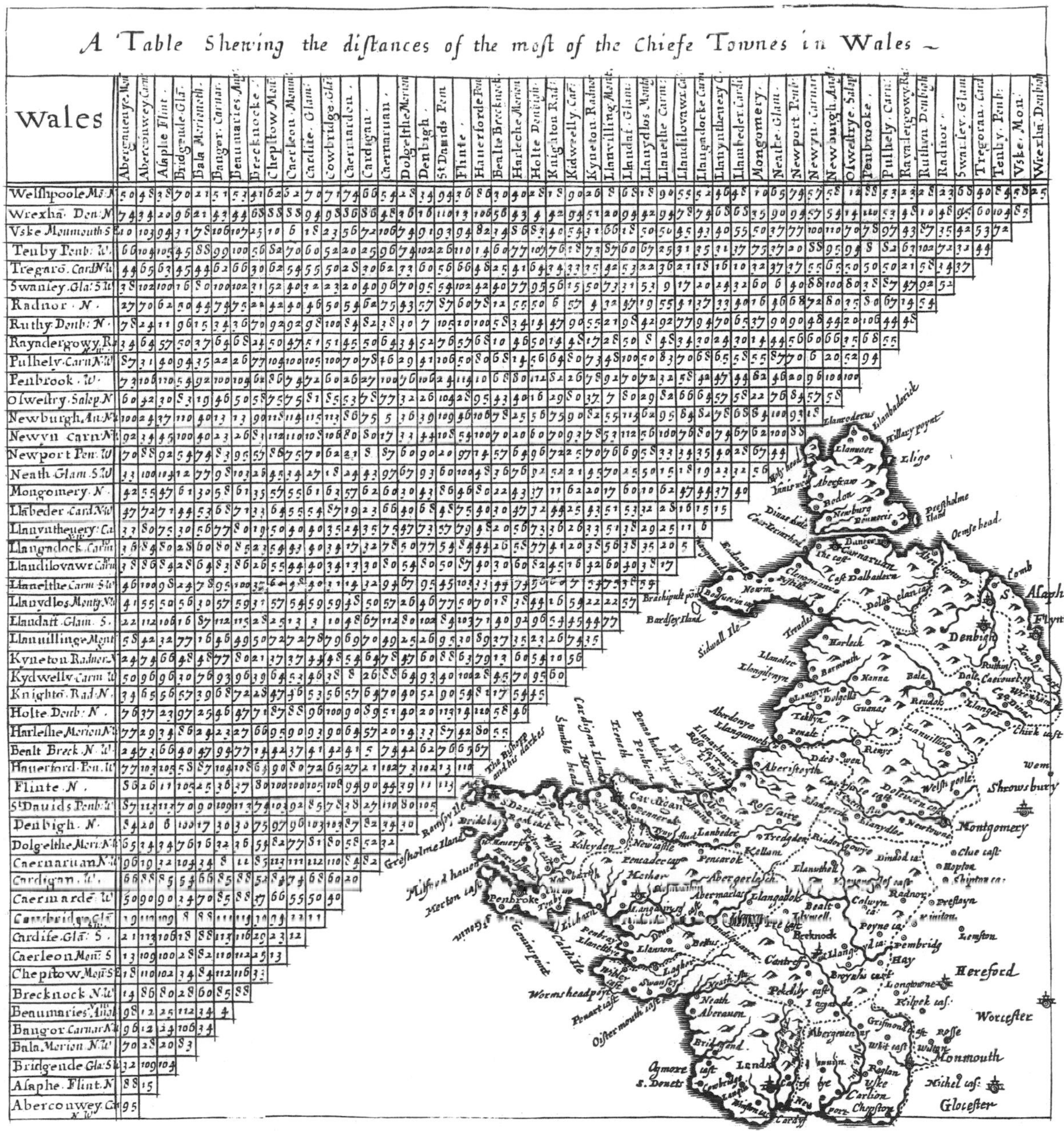

Wales

Row labels (left column, top to bottom):

- Welshpoole Mi: N
- Wrexhā Den: N
- Vske Monmouth S.
- Tenby Penb: W.
- Tregaro Card N.
- Swanley Gla: S.
- Radnor N.
- Ruthy Denb: N.
- Raynder gowy R.
- Pulhely Carn N.
- Penbrook W.
- Olwestry Salop N.
- Newburgh An: N.
- Newyn Carn N.
- Newport Pen: W.
- Neath Glam S.
- Mongomery N.
- Llabeder Card N.
- Llanynthevery Ca:
- Llangadock Carm
- Llandilovawr Carm
- Llanelthe Carm S.
- Llanydlos Monty N.
- Llandaff Glam S.
- Llanuillinge Mont
- Kyneton Radnor
- Kydwelly Carm W.
- Knighto Rad N.
- Holte Denb N.
- Harlethe Merion N.
- Benlt Breck N. W.
- Hauerford Pen W.
- Flinte N.
- S. Dauids Penb W.
- Denbigh N.
- Dolg: elthe Meri N.
- Cnernaruan N. W.
- Cardigan W.
- Caermarde W.
- Cambridge Gla:
- Cardife Gla: S.
- Caerleon Mon: S.
- Chepitow Mon S.
- Brecknock N. W.
- Benumaries Ann
- Bangor Carnar N.
- Bala Merion N. W.
- Bridgende Gla: S.
- Alaphe Flint N.
- Aberconwey C. N. W.

No. 12   Jacob Van Langeren map of Wales, Simmons, 1635 (1643)

Joan (John) Blaeu, 1596-1673

A famous firm of Dutch cartographers and publishers was established in the late 1500's by Willem Janszoon Blaeu in Amsterdam. Blaeu was a maker of globes and scientific instruments and purchased some of his early map plates from Jodocus Hondius. From this small beginning was to emerge one of the largest and most prolific map publishing houses of the seventeenth century.

Willem's two sons, Joan and Cornelius, both entered the family business and in 1630 the firm published its first world Atlas, bound in a single volume. This was increased to two volumes in 1635 and to three in 1640.

In 1645 Joan Blaeu published a county Atlas of England and Wales as part of his *Atlas Novus*, with maps based mainly on the earlier researches of Saxton and Speed. In a number of instances, Blaeu grouped several Welsh counties together on a sheet. The Atlas was a masterpiece with a balanced style and calligraphic quality that has never been surpassed. Ornamental cartouches were used in support of the scroll which carried the name of the county. Frequently the atlases were hand coloured before they were issued, often highlighted in gold. The pictorial elegance of some of them has to be seen to be believed.

The colour key for the armorials in the Atlas appears to have been taken from Speed's first edition of his *Theatre of the Empire of Great Britain*. Due to an engraver's error in the Atlas, the Arms of the Welsh Princes on the 'Achievement' page were given the wrong colour indications, showing four Or (gold) lions on a Gules (red) field. This mistake was later noticed and a coloured copy of the Speed 1614 edition, now in the British Library (maps C7 c19) carries the correct red and gold quarterings to the field of the shield. It seems that this correction was not brought to the notice of the Blaeus' and as late as 1662 they were still issuing contemporarily coloured maps of Wales with gold lions displayed on a red field. Blaeu maps that carry this colouring error are almost certain to have been coloured at the time the Atlas was issued.

The map of Hampshire illustrated appeared in the 1648 edition of the Atlas. The fine ornamental cartouche is embellished with the produce of the county and its agriculture, including fish, sheep and cattle. The Royal Arms are placed within the Garter in the upper right hand corner. Eight shields carry the arms of the Earls of Winchester and Southampton, and a ninth is engraved in outline but carries no armorial. A variety

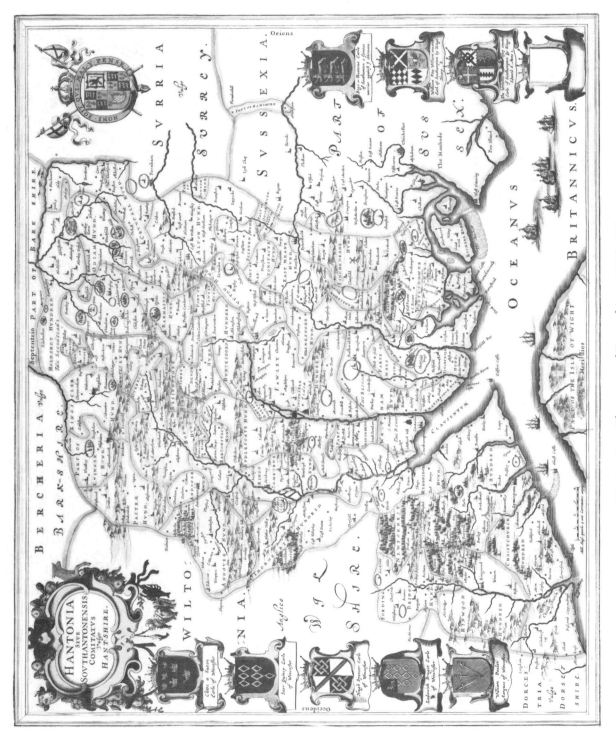

No. 13   Joan Blaeu map of Hampshire, 1645 (1648)

of sailing craft, some moored, others under full sail, embelish Southampton water. The fine contemporary hand-colouring displays the usual Blaeu quality, and the shading (hatchering) around the coastline is uncoloured. Some modern colourists seem determined to apply a blue wash over these shaded areas which is a pity.

There is a fairly heavy demand from the buying public for this particular map and good examples are difficult to find.

The Blaeus output was prodigious and the atlases sold in many countries. Editions in 1645 were issued with both Latin and French text. There were two Latin editions in 1646, as well as French and German ones. A Dutch edition appeared in 1647 and in 1648 there were Latin, French, German and Dutch editions. In 1659 came the first Spanish edition (rare) to be followed in 1662 with Latin, French and Spanish editions. The final edition in French appeared in 1667. Tragically their premises caught fire in 1672 and it is thought much of the plant and irreplaceable copper printing plates were destroyed. Little is known of the firm after this date.

Perhaps it should be pointed out that some Blaeu maps are signed Jonassonius Guilielmus or Jans Zeen Willems, and this signature can be confused with that of Jan Jansson who sometimes used the Latin form Janssonius Joannes, or Janssonium Joannem. We look at Jansson's work overleaf.

At the time of writing some examples of Blaeu county maps are not difficult to obtain and are less expensive than their Speed counterparts. However, their decorative merit and cartographic excellence is being increasingly appreciated and they will soon be scarce.

Size: $16\frac{3}{8}$ inches × $19\frac{3}{8}$ inches   Rating 3
          (416mm × 492mm)

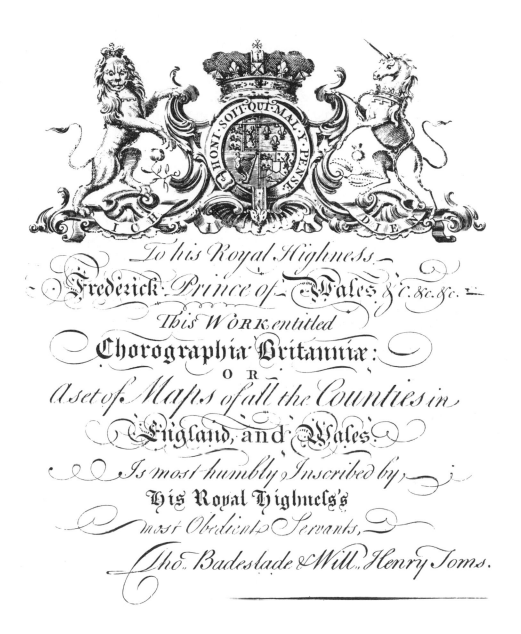

To his Royal Highness

Frederick Prince of Wales &c. &c. &c.

This WORK entitled

Chorographia Britanniæ:

OR

A set of Maps of all the Counties in

England, and Wales

Is most humbly Inscribed by,

His Royal Highness's

most Obedient Servants,

Tho. Badeslade & Will. Henry Toms.

Jan Jansson, 1588-1664

This important Dutch cartographer, printer and publisher was a contemporary and rival of Willem Blaeu. He worked for a time with his brother-in-law Jodocus Hondius, and his sons Jodocus and Henricus. Jansson and Hondius continued the publication of the Mercator Atlas and an English edition was published between 1633 and 1636 containing some 196 maps, including the Lhuyd map of Wales.

Jansson was anxious to produce an atlas of the British Isles before his great rival, Blaeu, but Blaeu managed to publish in 1645, Jansson the following year.

This very decorative map of Ireland has a large title cartouche in Latin and English, surmounted by the arms of Ireland. Above, in the upper left hand corner are the Royal arms with supporters. On the right hand side of the map is part of the west coast of Scotland and England and Wales, displaying the Arms of Scotland and Richard I. The map is typical of the attractive swash lettering that appears on many of Jansson's maps.

Early maps of Ireland are uncommon. The first atlas to contain a map of the country appeared in the *Additamentum to the Theatrum Orbis Terrarum*, in 1573. Ortelius appears to have copied this from Mercator's map of the British Isles which was also used for the map of Ireland in *Camden's Britannia*. Jansson's map was, however, based on Speed as were those of Blaeu, Vrints and Blome.

Jansson issued a French edition of the Atlas in 1646, French, Dutch and German editions in 1647, German and Dutch editions in 1649, French, German and Dutch editions in 1652. A single Dutch edition followed in 1653, a French edition in 1656, and a final Latin edition in 1659.

The maps from this Jansson Atlas appear to be less common than one would imagine, perhaps because the published editions were smaller than those of Blaeu.

Jansson died in 1664 and the business passed to his son-in-law Janssonius Waeberghe. Waeberghe himself died in 1681 and the stock and equipment were sold at auction. Many of his printing plates for the British maps were acquired by Peter Schenk who, together with Gerard Valk, continued to issue them in sheet form with a new imprint, but without text.

Size: 15 inches × 19⅝ inches   Rating 3
    (381mm × 498mm)

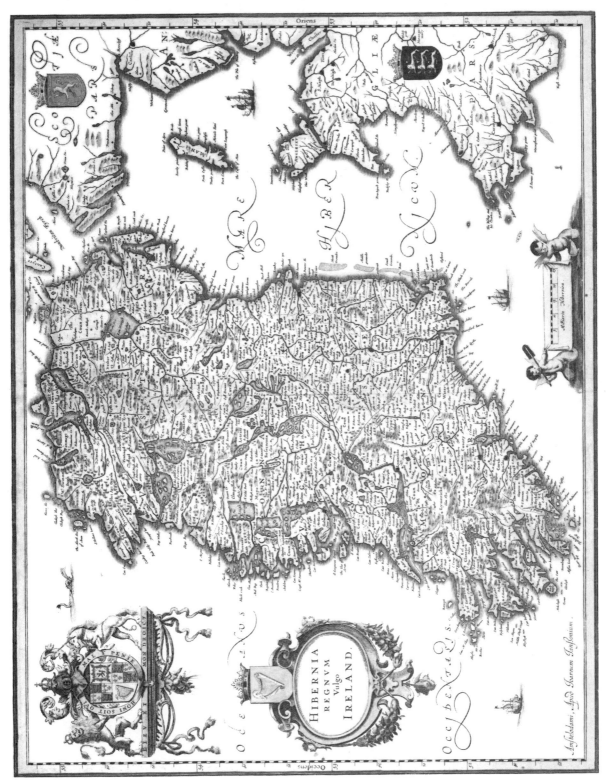

No. 14　Jan Jansson map of Ireland, 1646 (1659)

Richard Blome, 1641-1705

This Reformation period map-maker and publisher issued his first important cartographic work containing maps of the British Isles in 1673. The work was known as Blome's *Britannia* and contained some forty maps of the English counties including a general map of Scotland, one of Ireland and one of the Isle of Wight. Wales received scant treatment with two maps only, one of North and one of South Wales.

The Dictionary of National Biography describes Blome as 'a publisher and compiler of some celebrity, who by the aid of subscriptions adroitly levied, issued many splendid works'. He started life as an heraldic painter and on becoming a publisher used the advance subscription method in order to finance his projects. Of his published works outside the cartographic field *'The Gentlemen's Recreation'* is undoubtedly the best known. The book carries some of the earliest illustrations published of British field sports and its illustrations were prepared by some of the leading engravers of the day.

Many people appear to have mixed feelings about Blome and his contribution to the development of British map-making. Whilst it is true that he often copied the work of others, he made the mistake of being critical of the people whose work he chose to emulate. His comments about Camden's *Britannia* was that "it was a very dear book, scarce much out of print and never likely to be reprinted" John Speed's maps are described as "the best yet extant, which hath occasioned them to be so well approved of, that with usage they are, or soon will, become useless." He then proceeds to produce an atlas copied from Speed's earlier work!

Blome's map of Somerset is dedicated to the Rt. Hon. Maurice Berkeley, Baron Berkeley of Rathdowne, whose arms appear within a large ornamental cartouche in the top right hand corner of the map. The county title is positioned lower right, with a table of the hundreds in the left hand corner. The map is undated and has no scale or engraver's signature. One of the maps in this series was engraved by Wenceslaus Hollar who was also responsible for a number of the maps in the smaller publication 'Speed's Maps Epitomiz'd'. Hollar's fame as an etcher is well known in the world of print-collecting. An example of his cartographic engraving would be an interesting and valuable addition to any map collection.

Size: $9\frac{1}{2}$ inches × $13\frac{1}{8}$ inches   Rating 3
(242mm × 333mm)

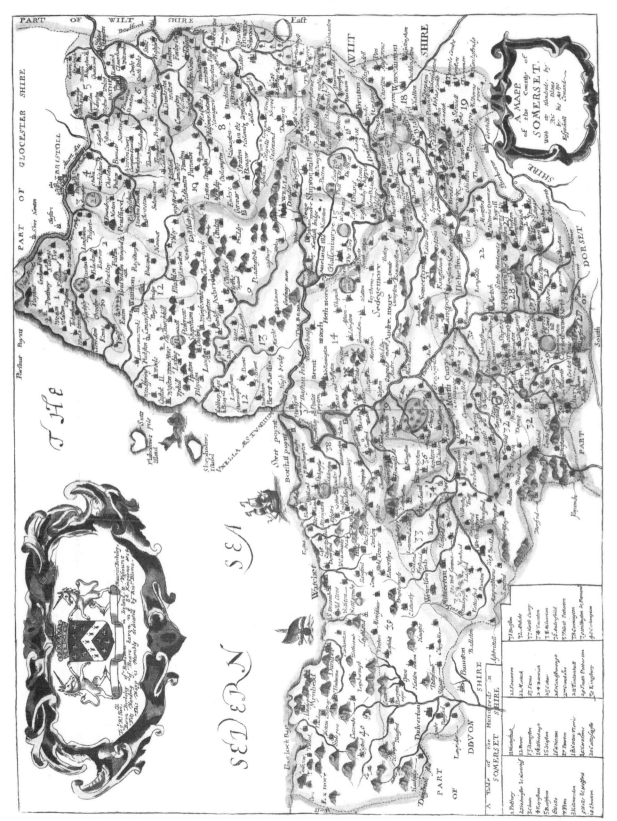

No. 15   Richard Blome map of Somerset, 1673

John Ogilby, 1600-1675

John Ogilby is regarded by some collectors as the most important name in British cartography since Christopher Saxton. He was born in Edinburgh in 1600, destined to become a man of many parts. He started life as a dancing teacher and followed this with a short career as tutor to the children of the Earl of Stafford.

He then went to Dublin where he ran a theatre, with some success, until the Civil War in 1641.

He nearly lost his life in the Irish troubles and returned to London penniless. After a period in Cambridge as a literary translater, he found favour at Court and was responsible for organising the Coronation Revels. He returned again to Dublin where he built his own theatre, which had to close due to a dispute. He then came back to London and set up a business as a printer and publisher, only to have his premises destroyed by the Great Fire of London in 1666.

After the fire he was appointed as one of four 'sworn viewers' who were ordered to survey those parts of the city that had been destroyed, in order to establish the rights of land ownership in the devastated areas. As a result of these researches a survey plan was published in 1667 on a scale of about twenty-five inches to the mile. Possibly as a result of this undertaking, the King appointed him Royal Cosmographer and Geographic Printer. Encouraged by the King's interest in the project, Ogilby started to prepare a three volume work *Britannia*, the first volume of which was to contain a series of maps depicting the roads of England and Wales. The work contained a hundred strip road-maps and was published in 1675. Unfortunately, Ogilby died in the year of publication of this volume, and the remaining two volumes were never completed.

This new Atlas was possibly the most important British cartographic achievement of the century and was used as a source of reference by many publishers, who, by the 1700's were producing regional and county maps showing roads for the first time.

Each of the strips carries a directional compass rose and distances are marked in miles and furlongs on a scale of 1 inch to the mile. All carry a remarkable amount of detail, including rivers, bridges, hills, county boundaries, unfenced roads, etc. Ogilby can also claim to have established the Statute Mile of 1,760 yards as the national unit of measurement, for, until the publication of his Atlas, there were no less

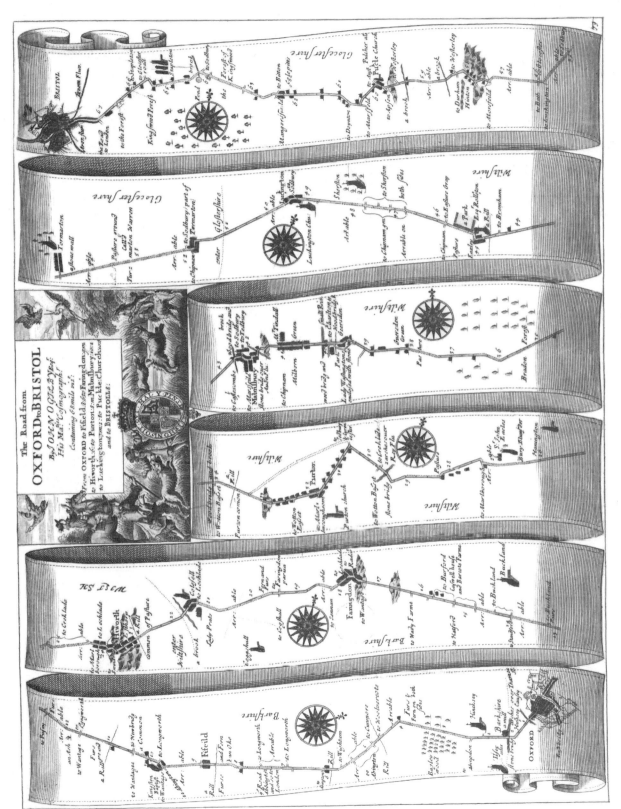

No. 16   John Ogilby road-map Oxford to Bristol, 1675 (1698)

In the Delineation or Decyphering these Roads upon Copper=Sculptures:

1. We have Projected them upon imaginary Scrolls, the *Initial City* or *Town* being always at the Bottom of the outmost Scroll on the Left Hand; whence your *Road* ascends to the Top of the said Scroll; then from the Bottom of the next Scroll ascends again, thus constantly ascending till it terminate at the Top of the outmost Scroll on the Right Hand, as by the Succession of Figures representing the Miles, most plainly appears.

2. The *Road* it self is express'd by double Black Lines if included by Hedges, or Prick'd Lines if open; but if the *Road* be describ'd altogether by Black Lines or Prick'd Lines throughout the whole Plate, then the Distinction aforesaid of En-clos'd and Open is omitted.

3. The *Scale* by which the said *Road* is Protracted, is according to one Inch to a Mile, or the 63'360th. Part of a Mile; the said Miles being exprest by double Points, and numbred by the Figures 1, 2, 3, &c. Each subdivided into 8 Furlongs, represented by the single Points included between the said double Ones.

4. The several Deviations or Turnings out of the *Road* to adjacent Places on ei-ther Hand, are exprest by a short double Line, and are generally inscrib'd, *to such a Place*, and sometimes the reputed Distance of the said Place in Miles is likewise signify'd by Figures affixt.

5. *Capital Towns* are describ'd *Ichnographically*, according to their Form and Ex-tent; but the *Lesser Towns* and *Villages*, with the *Mansion Houses*, *Castles*, *Churches*, *Mills*, *Beacons*, *Woods*, &c. *Scenographically*, or in *Prospect*.

6. *Bridges* are usually noted with a Circular Line like an Arch, but are general-ly imply'd where the *Rivers* or *Brooks* crost are not drawn through the *Road*.

7. *Rivers* are *Decypher'd* by a treble wav'd Line or more, and the lesser *Rills* or *Brooks* by a single or double Line, according to their Eminency.

8. *Ascents* are noted as the *Hills* in ordinary *Maps*, *Descents* e contra, with their *Bases* upwards.

9. Whatever is posited upon or within the Scroll, is presum'd to bear the same Scale as the *Road* it self.

10. The several Inclinations of the *Road* to the one or th' other Hand, are na-turally express'd accordingly, and the *Points of Bearing* are Collected from the pe-culiar Compass of each Scroll, the *Flower=de=luce* shewing the North; and when a Compass is repeated in the self same Scroll, a straight transverse Line expresses to what Part of the Scroll either of the said Compasses belong.

No. 17   Excerpt from Ogilby Road Atlas, 1675

66

than three different length 'miles' in use.

There was, of course, a great demand for the Atlas and two further issues were published in 1675, and another in 1698. Except for the original edition all the maps are numbered in the bottom right hand corner from 1 to 100. They were not again published after 1698.

Size: 12¾ inches × 17 inches   Rating 3
       (324mm × 432mm)

William Redmayne, fl.1676

The first set of playing cards bearing maps of the English and Welsh counties is thought to have been produced by William Bowes in 1590. The 52 thumbnail county maps that appeared on the cards were based on the general map of England and Wales in Saxton's Atlas. Robert Morden, the cartographer and publisher, also produced a fine set of cards in 1676 and William Redmayne, a stationer of the Crown on Addle Hill, issued his own pack later that same year.

On the map of Montgomeryshire, the quality of the engraving and the layout of the card is far less detailed than its Morden counterpart.

The county is represented by a dotted outline and the only town shown on the map is Montgomery. The card in question is the four of Spades. The text reads as follows 'Is bounded on ye North with Denbyshire, on ye East with Shrop-shire, on ye South with Radnor and Cardigan And on ye West with Merionethshire. Its Form like a Pear, with High Hills, Plenty of Springs, Severne ye Chife River its Hilly and yealds store of Cattel, Especially Horses . . . Montgomery-Town and 5 more of Trade. Montgomery its Latitude is 53 Degrees and Longitude 17. It is an Earldome and hath 7 Hundreds, 6 Market-Towns and 47 Parrishes.'

The cards were issued three times between 1676 and 1712. Redmayne published the two earlier editions and a new set was engraved for the second edition making them fairly easy to identify. He also reduced his price from 1/- per pack to 6d, doubtless due to the competition created by Morden. In his original issue, the suitmarks were engraved in outline and the colour blocked in, possibly by stencil. For the second edition the outline of the suitmarks was cross hatched for the black suits and given vertical engraved lines for the red suits. The edition of 1712 appears to have been taken from the same plates, but with the addition of a decorative border to the edges of the cards. This same design appears on cards issued by John Lenthill around 1712 and it seems likely that this final edition was published by him. Lenthill is thought to have been the largest supplier of playing cards in the country at that time.

The output of playing cards in Britain was seriously curtailed during Cromwellian times, when both cards and play were regarded as sinful. This puritanical attitude resulted in the wholesale destruction of many fine sets of cards. They were replaced by packs of an instructional or educational nature, embracing geography, history and similar subjects.

MONTGOMERY SHIRE

Is bounded on ÿ North. wᵗʰ Den-by-ſhire. on ÿ Eaſt with Shrop-ſh-ire. on ÿ South. with Radnor and Cardgan.

And on ÿ Weſt. with Merioneth-ſhire. Its Form like a Pear. with High Hills. plenty of Springs. Seve-rns ÿ Chiſe River is. Hilly yealds ſtore of Cattel. Eſpecially Horſes.

Montgomery-Town and 5 more are of Trade. Montgomery its La-titude is 53. Degrees and Long-itude 17.
It is an Earldome   and hath 7. Hundreds. 6. Market-Town s, and 47. Parriſhes.

No. 18   William Redmayne playing card map of Montgomeryshire, 1676 (1712)

These novelty cards became quite popular and are keenly sought by collectors of playing cards, for the subject now enjoys a collecting vogue all its own. The Redmayne and Morden geographical cards are typical examples of this variation.

Any card from this series will make an interesting addition to a collection, but they are rare and likely to be expensive.

Size: $3\frac{1}{2}$ inches $\times$ $2\frac{1}{16}$ inches   Rating 2
     (89mm $\times$ 51mm)

Printing in the Seventeenth Century

Captain Greenvile Collins, fl.1690

In 1676 Captain Greenvile Collins was commissioned by King Charles II to chart the coasts of Great Britain. He produced his *Great Britain's Coasting Pilot* in 1693, the first original Sea-Atlas to be produced by an Englishman.

Little is known about the life of this naval captain except that he was a Younger Brother of Trinity House when he undertook the King's commission.

He commenced the survey in 1681, taking seven years to complete it. As the charts he compiled were engraved and printed, so they were sold, some 48 charts on forty-five sheets. The complete work was first published in 1693 but re-issued many times during the eighteenth century.

Captain Collins is represented by his chart of Milford Haven, a fine dark impression, engraved by James Moxon, although the large decorative cartouche bearing the Royal arms (without Supporters) carries the signature of James Collins as engraver. The cartouche occupies almost a quarter of the chart's surface area. An oval panel carries a dedication to 'His Grace Henry, Duke of Beaufort, and Earle of Worcester, Baron Herbert of Chepstoll, Ragland and Gower, Lord President and Lord Lieut. of Wales, etc.' The panel is surrounded by cherubs making merry, others clutching fish. Two workmen of the period, one holding a pick-axe, the other a spade, sit either side, together with various animals and birds.

In the lower right hand corner of the chart is a group of figures in the dress of the period, together with Justice blindfolded, holding scales and a sword. The man opposite carries a key and a cane. Beneath the figures is a panel containing the scale in English Miles.

A compass rose is positioned in the lower left hand corner and three sailing vessels add to the chart's highly decorative appearance.

The Atlas was re-issued many times between the first edition and the last one in 1764 and as some of the later copies are pale impressions, they are usually rejected by serious collectors.

Size: $17\frac{5}{8}$ inches × $22\frac{1}{2}$ inches   Rating 3
(447mm × 572mm)

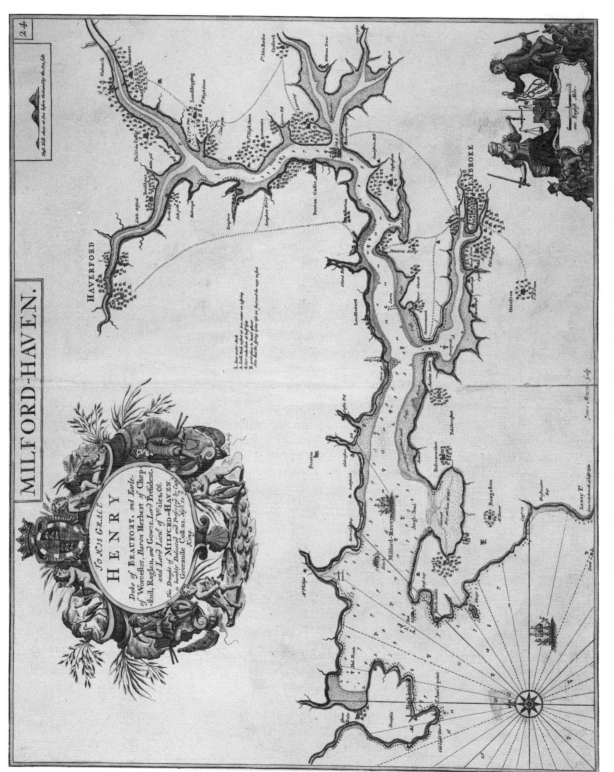

No. 19   Captain Greenvile Collins chart of Milford Haven, 1693 (1723)

John Seller, fl.1658-1698 d

John Seller was a cartographer, map seller, and scientific instrument maker with business premises at The Mariner's Compass, in Wapping. In 1671 he published the first volume—Book 1, of a projected sea-atlas which he named *The English Pilot*. In the same year he was appointed Hydrographer to King Charles II. He published Book 2, together with portions of Book 3 and 4 in 1672, but by 1680 this venture had been abandoned and he had sold the rights of these maritime publications.

He then embarked, with others, upon a national survey of England and Wales, for a projected atlas to be known as the *Atlas Anglicanus*, but this was likewise abandoned in 1693, when only six of the county maps had been prepared.

His next project was his *Anglia/Contracta* published in 1694/5. This small Atlas contained individual maps; based on Speed, of all the counties of England and Wales. The English maps each had a page of descriptive text, but for some reason this information was not provided for their Welsh counterparts.

Seller is represented by his map of Glamorganshire. The county title, scale and a compass device being the only embellishments, although the map has a grid marked upon it, an innovation first introduced by Norden. These small maps are becoming increasingly popular with collectors, but early issues are not easy to find. Further editions of the Atlas were published in 1696, 1697 and 1703. The maps were also used to illustrate *Camden's Britannia Abridged* in 1701, as well as by Francis Grose for *The Antiquities of England and Wales* which was published between 1773-1787, using reworked and altered map plates with descriptive text beneath the maps.

Size: $4\frac{1}{4}$ inches $\times$ $5\frac{5}{8}$ inches
  (107mm $\times$ 143mm)

Rating 3

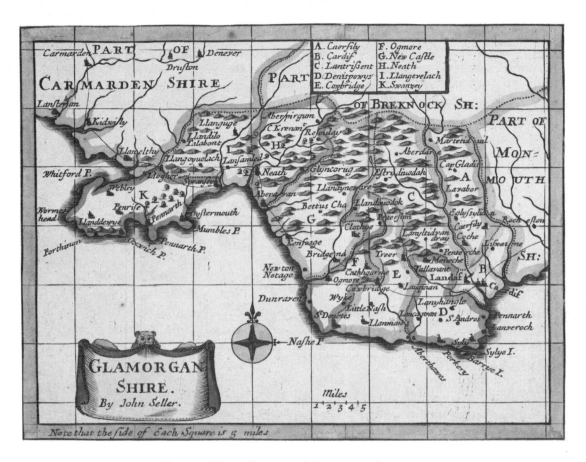

No. 20   John Seller map of Glamorganshire, 1695

Robert Morden, fl.1650-1703 d

After the publication of the final editon of *Camden's Britannia* in 1637, various abridgements appeared over the years, but the work was not published again until 1695 when Dr. Edmund Gibson (later Bishop Gibson) undertook the various editorial revisions. The new work contained fifty maps, mostly of the English counties with maps prepared by Robert Morden.

Morden was a bookseller and publisher working from premises in London's Cornhill when the Atlas was issued, and is represented with his map of Ireland illustrated.

The title is contained within an ornamental cartouche in the top left hand corner of the map. Two scales, representing Irish and English miles, appear in the lower right hand corner, otherwise the map is without embellishment.

It is interesting to compare this relatively accurate example by Morden with three other maps of Ireland. The one in *Camden's Britannia* after Mercator is very inaccurate as far as the north and west coasts are concerned. Speed's version, later copied by Jansson and later by Blome, provides us with two identical maps, the latter published in 1673, only twenty years before the updated Morden example illustrated. Morden's map issued in 1695 was doubtless influenced by the publication of Sir William Petty's *Hiberniae Delineatio* in 1685, (the first atlas of Ireland) which Morden helped to produce. Morden's was the first English County Atlas to include roads.

Most of the maps bear the names of Abel Swale and Awnesham and John Churchill which appear in the lower right hand corner of the map. They were the three highly respected publishers who financed the work and doubtless commissioned Morden to provide the maps. Subsequent editions of the work appeared in 1722, 1753 and 1772.

Similar examples are fairly common at the present time.

Size: $16\frac{1}{4}$ inches × $13\frac{1}{2}$ inches   Rating 3
    (412mm × 343mm)

No. 21   Robert Morden map of Ireland, 1695 (1722)

Schenk and Valk, fl.1695

The closing years of the seventeenth century witnessed a period of stagnation as far as British cartographic development was concerned, apart from the publication of Ogilby's Road Atlas and the Sea Atlas of Captain Greenvile Collins. In Holland, the most important map publishing concerns of Blaeu and Janson were no longer in existence.

The Janson business had been acquired by Peter Schenk, a Dutch publisher and engraver. A few years later we find him associated with Gerald Valk, who was in business as a map and chart seller. Between them the two men re-issued many county maps from the earlier plates of Jansson and Blaeu. In addition, Schenk published a number of original maps engraved by himself.

The Map of South Wales was originally published in the Jansson *Novus Atlas/Magna Britannia*. This was re-issued bearing the Schenk and Valk imprint and is thought to have been published between 1685 and 1695. Most maps carrying their imprint were usually issued singly, not in atlas form. Apart from the imprint this map is identical to the earlier editions by Jansson as far as detail is concerned, but is without text on the reverse.

As maps of Jansson and Blaeu are represented in the collection, there may seem little point including an identical map that has been merely re-issued by another publisher. However, these Schenk and Valk maps are at present a good deal less expensive than their Jansson and Blaeu counterparts and enable the collector of modest means to acquire a representative map at a lower price.

Size: $16\frac{1}{8}$ inches $\times$ $20\frac{1}{4}$ inches   Rating 4
      (410mm $\times$ 514mm)

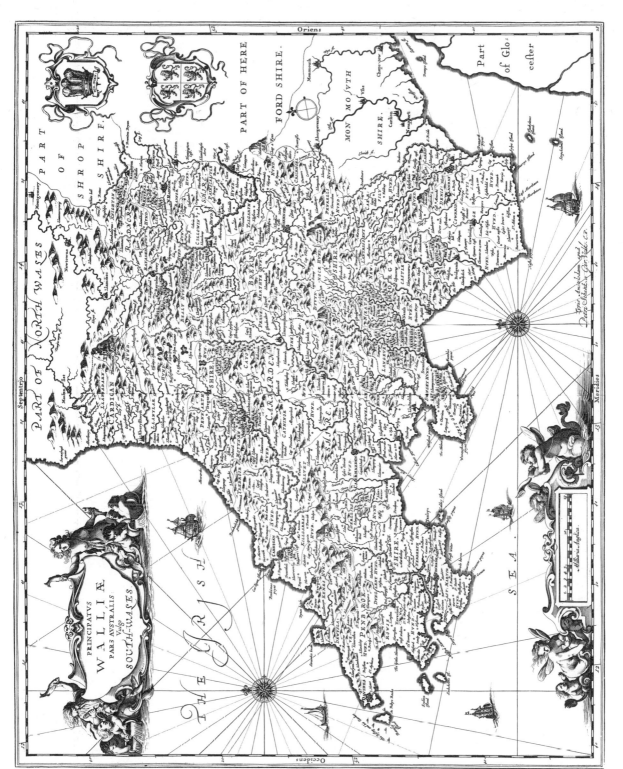

No. 22   Schenk and Valk issue of map of South Wales, 1646 (c.1695)

John Senex fl.1700-1740 d

Although John Ogilby's road Atlas introduced in 1675 was to prove a boon to the long distance traveller, its size and weight made it cumbersome and unwieldy for anyone not travelling by private coach.

In the early part of the eighteenth century, the coaching system of Britain was still in its infancy. Long distance travel, both dangerous and exhausting, had often to be undertaken on horseback. The demand for a smaller and lighter publication was obvious, but nearly half a century elapsed before John Senex published a near pocket version of Ogilby entitled *An Actual survey of all the principal Roads of England and Wales.*

This octavo work was published in 1719, in two volumes price five shillings and sixpence. Senex wrote that his Atlas, though based on Ogilby ". . . was much improved and corrected . ." although a close and detailed inspection provides no evidence in support of this claim. Two editions of the Atlas were published before his death in 1740 and his widow continued the publication, that concluded with a French version in 1759.

Senex was one of the most prolific engravers and publishers of the early eighteenth century. He prepared a number of large scale maps of England, Scotland and Ireland, including a regional map embracing Surrey, Kent, Sussex, Hampshire and Berkshire. His finest achievement was a world atlas entitled *Modern Geography* published in 1725, containing thirty-four large folio maps. His series of town plans including Salisbury, Vienna, Paris, Amsterdam and Rome are now in great demand.

A catalogue issued by his widow Mary shortly after his death lists a variety of globes, celestial and terrestial and concludes with "A small Map of England for a Watch,—Price 3d."

Examples of his road-maps are not too difficult to find although the ones without the cartouche information are rather plain and uninteresting.

Size: $6\frac{1}{4}$ inches × $8\frac{1}{2}$ inches   Rating 3
     (158mm × 215mm)

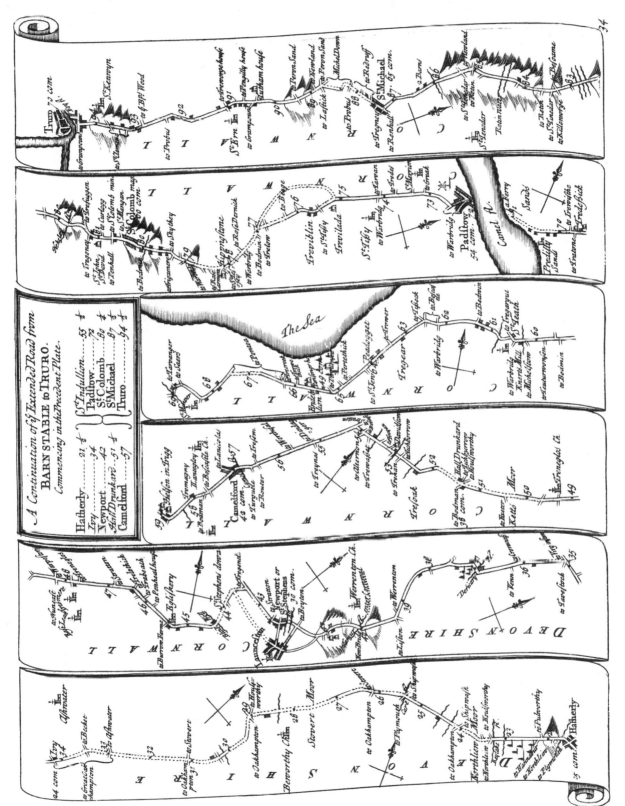

No. 23   John Senex road-map Barnstaple to Truro (part II) 1719

Thomas Gardner, fl. 1720

Following publication of the Senex road-atlas in 1719, Thomas Gardner issued a similar atlas later that same year, entitled *Pocket Guide to the English Traveller*. The Gardner, like the Senex, was a reduction of the Ogilby Atlas but the quality of the engraved work and general appearance of the maps are rather more attractive than those of Senex.

The map illustrated covers the road from Shrewsbury to Holiwell in Flintshire. It carries a dedication to Sir John Conway in a central panel, together with Gardner's name and details of the route to be followed. All the engraved detail is the same as Ogilby's apart from a variation in the shading of the hills. It is interesting to speculate why the Gardner Atlas was not re-issued when the less attractive Senex publication ran to eight editions. John Senex was of course better known and as a Fellow of the Royal Society must have enjoyed a wide circle of friends and acquaintances likely to be interested in a work of this kind. The publication in 1720 of another important miniature road atlas *Britannia Depicta* by Emanuel Bowen and John Owen was soon to provide even greater competition.

There is now an increasing demand for these smaller and less expensive road-atlases from collector's who have a particular interest in the growth of the country's roads. They form a vital link in the development of our roads from the time of the Restoration until the introduction of the near modern road maps of John Cary at the end of the eighteenth century.

Size: $7\frac{1}{8}$ inches × 11 inches   Rating 3
   (181mm × 279mm)

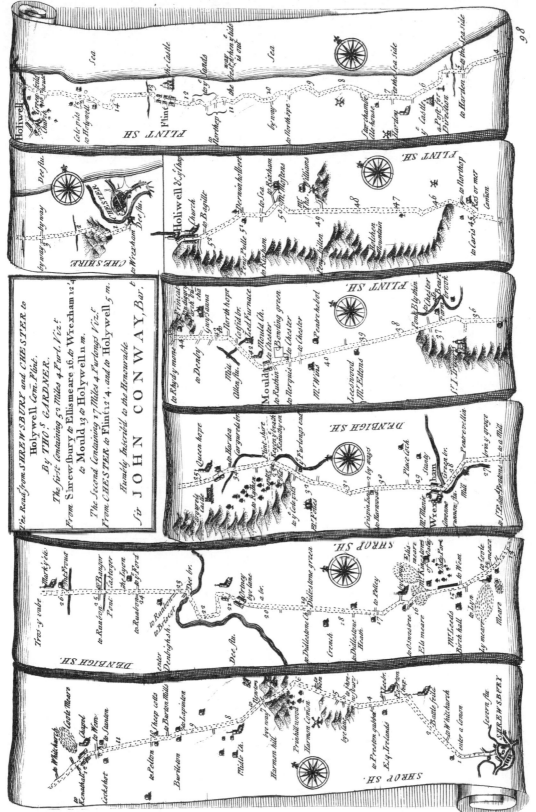

No. 24   Thomas Gardner road-map Shrewsbury to Holiwell, 1719

John Owen and Emanuel Bowen, fl.1750

Emanuel Bowen was one of the most skilled and prolific engravers of the eighteenth century. One of his earliest engraved works *Britannia Depicta* published in 1720, contained over two hundred road maps together with a miniature county map of each of the counties of England and Wales. It was an unusual feature of the Atlas that the maps were engraved on both sides of each page, and this resulted in a handier sized book with a corresponding reduction in thickness. Apart from the text, the backs of most line engraved maps were left blank.

Today, the maps are frequently supplied double glazed, that is to say with glass on the reverse side as well, thus the customer has a choice of two maps. Only rarely do the maps relate to the same road.

The publisher of the Atlas was a John Owen, hence the term Owen and Bowen to describe maps from the work. The Atlas was in great demand for a period of approximately forty years and twelve subsequent editions appeared between the first and final one in 1764. As mentioned elsewhere, the appreciation rate of this series of maps over the past three or four years has been remarkable. Although there were many editions, so many of the atlases have now been broken up for the maps, that a complete volume in good condition is likely to command a high price.

Owen and Bowen are represented with their map of Lincolnshire. A decorative and finely engraved cartouche above the map gives details of the road from Nottingham to Grimsby. Underneath appears details of the county, its size, climate, industry and commerce. It was this kind of interesting information that Bowen later incorporated on the face of his larger county maps which may account for their popularity with collectors.

Good examples are still not too difficult to obtain, but county maps, like the one illustrated, are likely to be considerably more expensive than those giving only the road detail.

Size: $7\frac{1}{4}$ inches $\times$ $4\frac{1}{2}$ inches   Rating 3
(184mm $\times$ 115mm)

The ROAD from NOTTINGHAM to GRIMSBY in LINCOLNSHIRE. Containing 50 Comp & 67½ Meas.d M.

From Nottingham

	Comp.	Meas.		Comp.	Meas.
to Newark	12	17½	to Stanton	40	54½
LINCOLN	24	31⅞	Briggesly	46	61'6
Walton	29	38½	Grimsby	50	67½
Market Raising	36	48⅜			

A MAP of LINCOLN SHIRE

No. 25   John Owen and Emanuel Bowen map of Lincolnshire, 1720

Herman Moll, fl.1720-1732 d

This Dutch cartographer, engraver and publisher is known to have worked in Britain in the late seventeenth century. His large output, which he personally engraved, included maps of many parts of the world and his map of "The Whole World" published in 1719, shows California as an island.

It is unfortunate that, apart from a series of maps based on Ireland, most of Moll's work on the British Isles was confined to some of the charts for the *Collin's Sea Atlas* and to his *New Description of England and Wales*, an Atlas of the English and Welsh counties published in 1724.

This map of Herefordshire comes from a first edition of the Atlas and illustrates a series of archeological antiquities on either side of the map's outer border. The county title is displayed in a plain window in the top right hand corner, with a list of the hundreds beneath. The hundreds are indicated by dotted lines and the roads are shown in considerable detail. The scale is positioned in the lower left hand corner. Although the Atlas was re-published in 1740, and again in 1753, the antiquities in the borders were omitted and this provides a useful means of identifying first editions, since none of the maps are dated.

The publication of Ogilby's *Britannia* coupled with influences which were about to turn Britain into an industrial society, were soon to be reflected in a demand for maps that were capable of providing accurate information for the traveller, without the embellishments of a more leisurely age. As we continue with our look at the maps of the eighteenth century, we shall see less and less of the fine calligraphy, the ornamental cartouches, and the colourful armorials that had played such a fascinating part in the development of map-making for more than two hundred years.

Viewed in this light, the Moll may seem to have little to commend it. However, I consider it of sufficient importance to be included in a collection because it reflects something of the changes that were taking place in the development of mapping in the eighteenth century. Copies are not too difficult to find at present.

Size: $7\frac{1}{2}$ inches $\times$ $10\frac{1}{16}$ inches   Rating 4
     (190mm $\times$ 255mm)

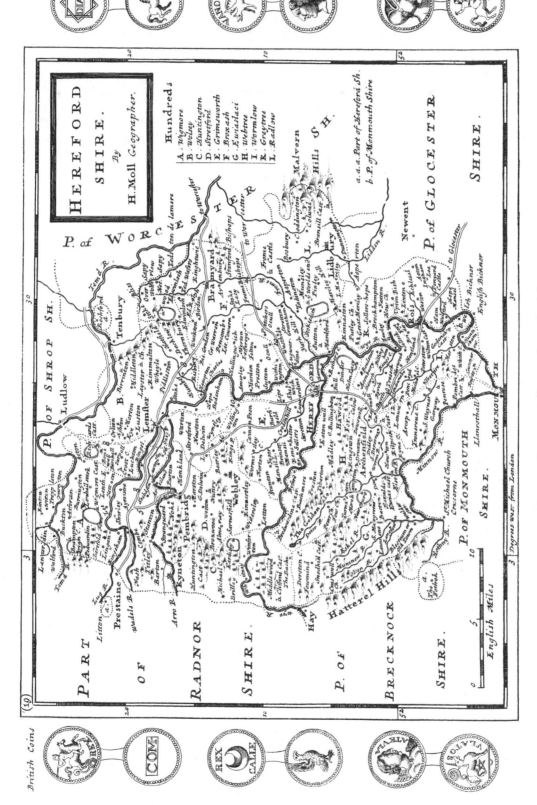

No. 26   Herman Moll map of Herefordshire, 1724

Badeslade and Toms fl.1719-1745

This interesting small Atlas was issued in 1742 by William Henry Toms (the engraver and publisher) and Thomas Badeslade, a surveyor colleague who prepared the maps for the series. The Atlas was entitled *Chorographia Britannia* and the preamble states that they were prepared ". . . by order and for use of his late Majesty King George I for his intended tour thro' England and Wales. . ." The forty-six maps are engraved to a high standard, detailing all towns and important villages together with roads and rivers, although the latter are exaggerated and somewhat out of proportion.

On the map of Middlesex the county title is placed outside the printed border. A compass indicator in the lower left hand corner is positioned above the scale. The surrounding areas are stippled and shaded in such a way that they have the effect of throwing the county into relief. Asterisks are used to indicate the number of members returned to Parliament.

A column on the left hand side contains interesting information on the county, its principal towns and markets and about the City of London, its buildings and institutions, including a reference to ". . . 32 Foreign Churches and 17 Publick prisons. . .":

Some of the maps in the Atlas are dated 1741 although the writer's copy appears to be a first edition and is dated 1742. There were several re-issues, with a second edition in 1745 and a final one in 1747.

Maps from the Atlas are quite scarce, possibly due the high mortality rate on these small atlases and also because the number of the various printings may have been limited.

Size: $5\frac{5}{8}$ inches $\times$ $5\frac{3}{4}$ inches   Rating 4
  (143mm $\times$ 146mm)

No. 27   Badeslade and Toms map of Middlesex, 1742

Thomas Osborne, fl.1740

In 1748, Thomas Osborne and others published a pocket Atlas entitled *Geographia Magnae Britanniae* containing 63 small county maps covering England, Wales and Scotland.

Osborne is represented with his map of Carnarvonshire. The county title is set in an engraved frame in the lower right hand corner of the map. Apart from the compass indicator, positioned in the Irish Sea, and the scale of miles the map is without decoration of any kind.

All the maps in the series are well engraved and show roads as well as the important towns and villages. The mountainous regions are depicted with the 'mole hill' type hills originally introduced by Saxton's engravers.

The Atlas was re-published in 1750 and was not issued again. Maps from it are quite scarce, perhaps because the editions were small. Osborne may have had doubts about its success, or else he lacked the necessary capital to promote the Atlas. The title page carries the names of no less than seven other publishers who joined him in the venture.

Size: $5\frac{3}{4}$ inches $\times$ $5\frac{3}{4}$ inches   Rating 3
    (147mm $\times$ 147mm)

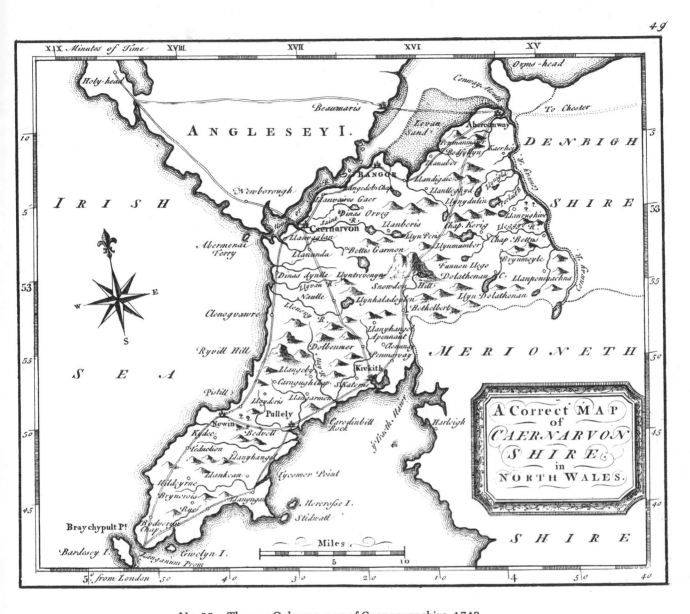

No. 28   Thomas Osborne map of Carnarvonshire, 1748

Thomas Kitchin & Thomas Jefferys
fl.1700-1750.

Map No. 29

In 1749 Kitchin and Jefferys published their *Small English Atlas* containing fifty maps of the counties of England and Wales. The Atlas was a very close copy of the one issued by Badeslade and Toms seven years earlier (Map No. 27). Kitchin had previously pirated the road atlas of John Senex in similar fashion.

The map of Gloucestershire illustrated is almost identical to the Badeslade map, Kitchin using the same engraving techniques with hatchering around the county to make it stand out from the map. There is a compass indicator in the top right hand corner of the map with a scale on the lower right hand side. Asterisks near certain towns indicate sitting members of Parliament and graduations of latitude and longitude have been inserted in the borders of the map.

Three further issues of the Atlas were published before the final edition of 1787 when the title was changed to an *English Atlas a Concise View of England and Wales.* Despite the number printed, maps from this Atlas are not easy to find.

Size: $4\frac{7}{8}$ inches $\times$ $5\frac{1}{4}$ inches   Rating 3
   (124mm $\times$ 133mm)

A Map of GLOCESTERSHIRE.

Glocestershire *Contains one City two Boroughs and 24 other Market Towns and sends eight Members to Parliament two for the County, two for the City of Glocester, and four for the two Boroughs.*

Glocester *City sends 2. Memb.ˢ Market Wed and Sat. Fairs March 25 June 24 Sept.ʳ 17 and Nov.ʳ 17.*

Cirencester *sends 2 Memb.ˢ Mark. M & F. Fairs July 7 Oct. 28 Easter Tues & Holy Thur.*

Tewkesbury *sends 2 Memb.ˢ Market Sat. Fairs Feb. 24 May 3 June 11 Aug 24 & Sep. 29.*

Dean *Market M. Fairs Sep. 29. & Easter Mo.*

Newent *Market F. Fairs Aug. 1. Mon. before Easter W. before Whitsunday F. after Sep. 8.*

Newnham *Mark. F. Fairs June 11 & Oct. 18.*

Marshfield *Market Tues. & Fair Oct. 13.*

Sodbury *Market Th. Fairs June 24 Holy Thurs. and 5ᵗʰ Sunday in Lent.*

Wickware *Mark. M. Fairs Mar. 25 & July 2.*

Thornbury *Market S. Fairs Aug. 15 Easter Mon. and Mon. before S.ᵗ Thomas's Day.*

Wotton *Market F. and Fair Sept.ʳ 14.*

Tetbury *Market Wed. Fairs July 22 and Ash Wednesday.*

Dursley *Market Thurs. Fairs April 25. and November 23.*

Barkley *Market W. and Fair May 3.*

Stanley *Market S. Fairs Novemb.ʳ 6 and Sat. after S.ᵗ Swithins Day.*

Stroud *Market Fri. Fairs May 1. and Aug. 10.*

Painswick *Market Tues. Fairs Sep. 8. and Whit-Tuesday.*

Lechlade *Market Tues. Fair Aug. 10.*

Fairford *Market Thurs. Fairs June 19 and November 1.*

North Lech *Market Wednesday.*

Cheltenham *Market Thurs. Fairs July 25 and Holy Thursday.*

Stow *Market Thursday Fairs May 1. and October 13.*

Winchcomb *Market Sat. Fairs April 25 and July 17.*

Moreton *Market Tues. disused.*

Campden *Market Wed. Fairs July 25 and Ash Wednesday.*

Minchinghampton *Market Tuesd. Fairs Oct.ʳ 18 and Trinity Monday.*

Colford *Mark.ᵗ Tu.*

No. 29   Thomas Kitchin & Thomas Jefferys map of Gloucestershire, 1749

Thomas Kitchin, 1718-1784

Map No. 30

The most important cartographic partnership of the eighteenth century was undoubtedly that between Thomas Kitchin and Emanuel Bowen. Both men were engravers of outstanding ability and individually prepared numerous maps and atlases. Later they decided on a joint venture which led to the publication in 1755 of the *Large English Atlas* containing forty-five maps of the English and Welsh counties. General maps of Scotland and Ireland were added in 1777. These county maps are regarded as the finest of the eighteenth century.

Some of Kitchin's earlier work is to be found in copies of the *London Magazine* dating from about 1748 and includes county maps of England, Wales, Scotland and Ireland. His maps are embellished with the traditional cartouches, often with an appropriate coat-of-arms. Kitchin's smaller maps were some of the most attractive produced during the mid-eighteenth century and they continued to appear in a number of atlases and other publications between 1749 and 1787.

His map of Haddingtonshire is typical of his work taken from the *London Magazine* and carries a small garlanded cartouche in the top right hand corner containing the county title. The map has a compass indicator in the top left hand corner and the scale in British Statute miles in the lower right hand. There are graduations of longitude and latitude within the printed border.

Kitchin combined with another well known engraver and publisher, Thomas Jefferys and together they produced the *Small English Atlas* in 1749, referred to in the preceeding chapter. This Atlas continued in publication several years after Kitchin's death in 1784.

The large Kitchin maps are now becoming scarce and expensive but examples of the smaller maps are not too difficult to find.

Size: 6½ inches × 8⅜ inches
(165mm × 213mm)

Rating 4

No. 30　Thomas Kitchin map of Haddingtonshire, 1750

George Bickham Snr., fl.1730-1771d

This unusual series of bird's eye-views of the English counties was prepared by George Bickham, one of the leading copper-plate engravers of the eighteenth century. They were intended to compliment the illustrations of his *British Monarchy* (1750) although individual maps were issued as early as 1743.

The one of Warwickshire illustrated appeared in an early bound copy of *British Monarchy*, circa 1754 and provides a good example of the quality copper-plate lettering styles for which Bickham was renowned.

The hilly vantage point presents an imaginary bird's eye-view across the county taking in the cities of Birmingham, Coventry and the county town of Warwick. Various agricultural implements and some of the produce of the county are depicted, together with a young man in the dress of the period. There is dedication to the Rt. Hon. Earl Brooke above the map. Recorded beneath the view is the mileage between Warwick and other important towns and villages in the county and also a list of the hundreds.

When the maps were re-published by Messrs. Laurie and Whittle in 1796, the title was changed to *A Curious Antique Collection of Birds-eye Views*, and the elaborately engraved lettering above and below the maps was replaced by the name of the county only.

The purist may choose not to include one of these examples in his collection, regarding them as prints rather than maps. Early examples with the lettering top and bottom are very difficult to find and are likely to be expensive.

Size: 9 inches × 5¾ inches
(228mm × 146mm)

Rating 2

A MAP of WARWICK SHIRE N West from LONDON
Humbly inscrib'd to y.ᵉ R.ᵗ Hon.ᵇˡᵉ Earl Brooke Lord Lieu.ᵗ of y.ᶜ County.

From London to Warwick 96. Principal towns from Warwick; to Atherston 24, Nuneaton 18,
Alcester 15, Pollsworth 28, Birmingham 28, Solihul 30, Coleshill 22, Southam 10, Coventry 10,
Stratford 10, Henly-Arden 8, Sutton-Cofield 36, Kyneton 12, Tamworth 38. Five Hundreds,
Barlichway, Knightlow, Hemlingford, Kyneton, The Liberty of Coventry.
According to Act of Parliam.ᵗ by G Bickham

No. 31   George Bickham Bird's Eye view of Warwickshire, 1750

John Rocque, fl.1750-1762 d

John Rocque was a French surveyor and engraver who came to Britain and settled here about 1735. Between this date and 1750 he was responsible for preparing and engraving a number of very detailed plans of large houses built by the gentry and wealthy merchant class.

He brought a number of new engraving techniques to this work in order to differentiate between cultivated land, gardens, heathland and the like. He also introduced a new method for shading hills which he depicted in plan with white tops varying the shading on the slopes, the closer the engraved lines the steeper the slope.

He prepared a series of large scale county maps employing these techniques which were more advanced than any previously published. The one illustrated is part of a four-sheet map of the county of Shropshire published in 1752, on a scale of one inch to the mile. He issued Middlesex in 1754 and an eighteen sheet map of Berkshire followed in 1761.

Rocque published the *Small British Atlas* in 1753 using maps that had previously appeared in the *English Traveller* (three volumes) of 1746. Subsequent editions were published in 1762, 1764 and 1769 with a new title *England Displayed* (edited by Russell and Price) where twenty-nine of the fifty-four maps are by Rocque, the remainder by Kitchin, Bowen and Rollos. His other published work includes a re-issue of Hollar's famous Quartermaster's map and several fine large scale town plans, including London and Bristol.

After his death in 1762 the business was conducted by his wife, Mary. Examples of his maps are not common and the large scale ones are now quite expensive.

Size: $23\frac{3}{4}$ inches $\times$ $20\frac{1}{4}$ inches   Rating 3
    (604mm $\times$ 514mm)

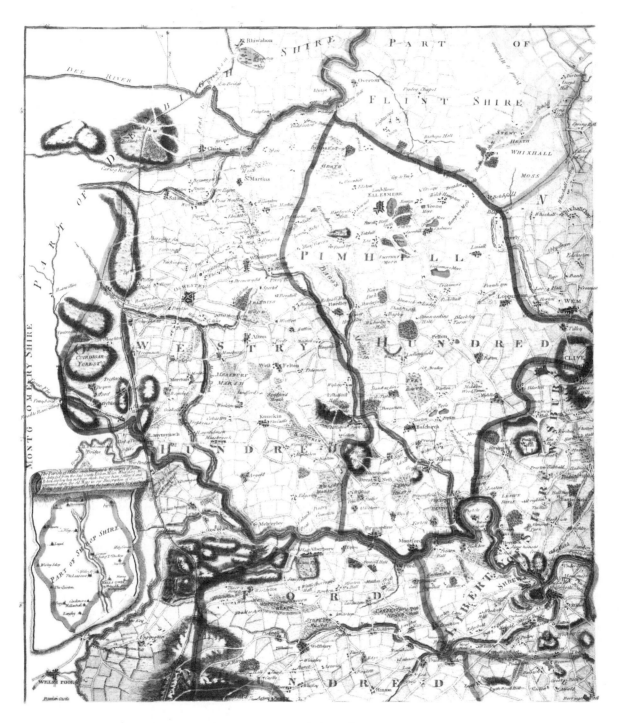

No. 32   John Rocque map of Shropshire (parts), 1753

99

G. Rollos, fl.1760

This British publisher, engraver and map-seller was one of four engravers who contributed map plates to *England Displayed*. The two volume work contains fifty-four maps from the gravers of Thomas Kitchin, Thomas Bowen, John Rocque and Rollos, the last named being represented in the collection with this map of Breckonshire.

This is an attractive map of somewhat larger format than many of its 18th century counterparts that appear in this work. There is an ornamental cartouche in the top right hand corner carrying the county title and the name G. Rollos, Geographer. The compass indicator is positioned on the left hand side of the map with the scale beneath.

The hills are depicted in plan, shaded in such a way on their eastern and western slopes that they convey an almost three dimensional effect when suitably hand coloured. The traveller intending to visit this county is left in no doubt as to the nature of the terrain he was about to encounter.

The roads are well detailed with mileage recorded between the important towns. The boundaries of the hundreds are indicated by dotted lines and there is the usual information on rivers, lakes, woods, etc.

Maps of this date display the plate mark as much as three-eighths or half an inch away from the map's outer border, perhaps an indication that the cost of copper sheet was less expensive as manufacturing methods improved.

In this period we find the same maps are starting to appear in different atlases and publications, often with the name of a previous publisher erased, making it difficult to establish from which work the map originates.

Examples of Rollos' maps are not common, only four of the fifty contained in this particular work were engraved by him.

Size: 8⅜ inches × 11⅜ inches   Rating 3
     (213mm × 289mm)

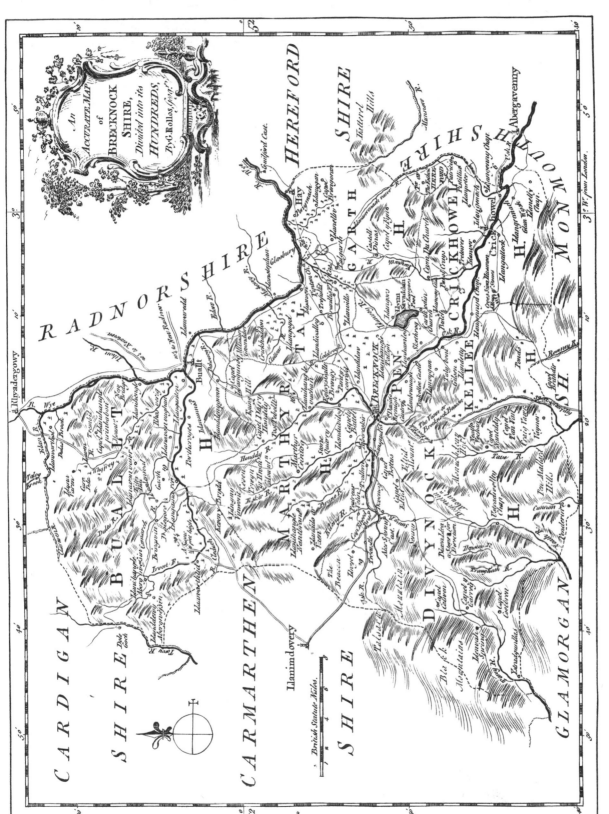

No. 33 G. Rollos map of Brecknockshire, 1760 (1768)

John Ellis, fl.1760-1790 d

John Ellis engraver and map-maker, produced a small Atlas of the counties of England and Wales with the title *Ellis's English Atlas*, published in 1766. The Atlas contained 48 maps with Welsh interest being catered for by the usual regional maps of North and South Wales.

Although it compares favourably with similar maps of that period, there is a particular reason for including it. The maps of North and South Wales appear on either side of the same leaf. On first sight each map appears to have a double plate mark, the paper having been passed twice through the printing press in order to receive the impressions. Except in the case of small road atlases, I have not before seen a copper-plate printing variation of this kind.

The Atlas was issued by Carington Bowles and Robert Sayer with editions in 1766, 1768 and 1777. In the original edition, 50 maps were listed but the Atlas contained only 48 maps. For a later edition, the maps were increased to 54. On my copy, the plate number for North Wales is given as 51, and for South Wales 52, which rather indicates that it could not have come from the first edition (48 maps).

There is a pleasing cartouche in the lower left hand corner, formed by a ruined archway on which appear the map's title and the name of the engraver, W. Palmer. A three masted sailing ship rides at anchor in Cardigan Bay, both it and the cartouche are uncoloured. There is a compass indicator and a key in the top left and right hand corners respectively. There is outline colour to the county boundaries, in what appears to be a contemporary hand. The map of South Wales, verso, has similar layout and colouring.

It would be interesting to know whether the complete Atlas was issued at some stage with an impression either side of the page in order to economise on paper. Much of our printing paper was still being imported from the continent at this time, when Britain seemed to be in constant conflict with the Dutch and French.

Maps from the Atlas are not too difficult to obtain, but an example of double printing such as the one described, is unusual.

Size: $7\frac{3}{4}$ inches × 10 inches   Rating 3
      197mm × 254mm

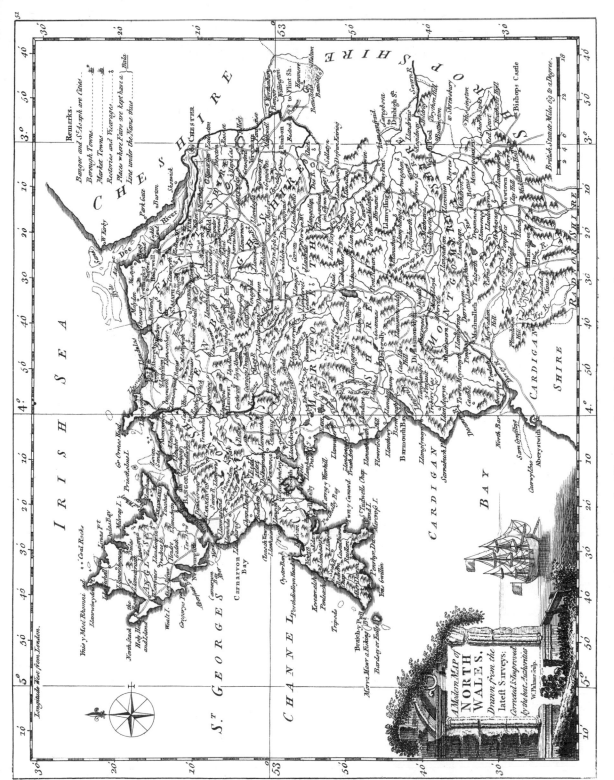

No. 34   John Ellis map of North Wales (verso South), 1766

Emanuel and Thomas Bowen, fl. 1750

Four cartographers of outstanding ability, contributed to the development and expansion of map-making in Britain during the eighteenth century. They were Emanuel Bowen, Thomas Bowen, Thomas Kitchin and John Cary.

We look first at the work of Emanuel and Thomas Bowen represented by their map of Durham from *Atlas Anglicanus* first published in 1767, and containing 45 maps of England and Wales. Maps from large atlases due to their size are difficult to reproduce in a book as small as this, but the format of the one illustrated is typical of that employed on the larger maps. Of the many issued by the Bowen's (and Kitchin), the *Anglicanus* is the smallest and is rare. Ten years were to elapse between the first edition in 1767 and a second and final one in 1777.

The maps were considerably up-dated compared with any previously published. The statement on the ornamental cartouche in the top left hand corner of the map reads ". . . with improvements not Inserted in any other Half Sheet Map Extant . . ." The map carries outline colouring to the hundreds only, as it was by that time the practice to leave the cartouche and the border of the map uncoloured. Roads and even the smaller villages are shown in great detail. Bowen employed at least five different lettering styles and this county map must be one of the finest examples of calligraphic copper engraving of the period. Much of its appeal is due to the interesting historical and topographical information that has been written into the map anywhere space permitted, an innovation used only by Bowen and Kitchin.

In the *Large Atlas*, the maps of the Welsh counties are half the size of the English ones, being engraved two to a page. They are less common than one might think despite the number of times the atlases were re-issued. They were published as follows, *Royal English Atlas*, 1762, 1778 and 1780, *Large English Atlas* 1755, 1763, 1777 and 1785, and *English Atlas* 1794 (this was a re-issue of Bowen's *Royal English Atlas* of 1762).

Size: $8\frac{5}{8}$ inches $\times$ $12\frac{1}{2}$ inches   Rating 3
(219mm $\times$ 318mm)

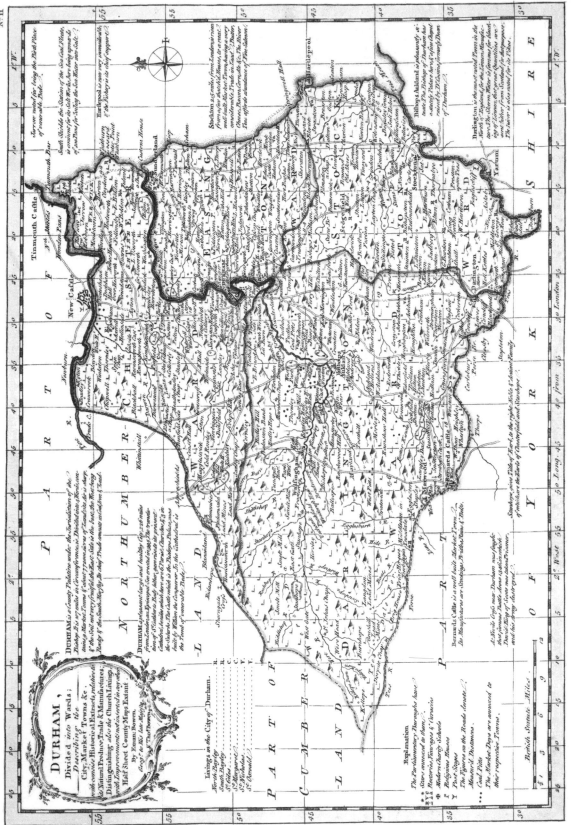

No. 35   Emanuel and Thomas Bowen map of Durham, 1767

Carington Bowles, 1724-1793

One of the rare small Atlases to be published in the eighteenth century was *Bowles's Pocket Atlas* issued in 1785, containing fifty-seven maps. At the time of writing only two complete copies of the Atlas are known, both in private hands.

Bowles is represented by his *Reduced Map of Anglesea Isle*. The map is well engraved and fairly plain in appearance. A compass indicator is placed in the upper right hand corner, the scale is towards the lower right hand. The following comments appear beneath the heading "Remarks" positioned near the lower left hand corner. "Beaumaris is the County Town and sends one member to Parliament. N.B. The Figures to the towns show their distance from London". Symbols representing market towns and villages are also included.

The Bowles family were prolific publishers throughout the eighteenth century. Thomas Bowles senior had two sons, Thomas and John. Carington Bowles was the son of John and published *Bowles's New Medium Atlas* in 1785. Other atlases published by the family include *Bowen's Large English Atlas*, *Atlas Minor* by Herman Moll and the 1764 edition of *Britannia Depicta*, the Owen and Bowen work previously mentioned. The chances of finding a map from this *Pocket Atlas* are remote.

Size: 5 inches × 6⅛ inches
    (127mm × 156mm)

Rating 1

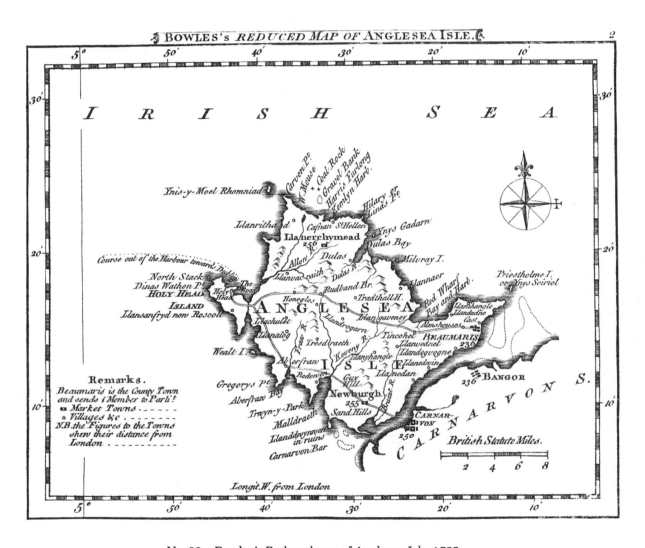

No. 36   Bowles's Reduced map of Anglesea Isle, 1785

107

Thomas Conder, fl.1780-1801

A series of small well-engraved copper plate maps executed by Thomas Conder appeared in various atlases and publications between 1786 and 1805. One of these was Henry Boswell's *Antiquities of England and Wales* published by Alexander Hogg in 1786 in which this map appears. Publisher Robert Wilkinson, successor to John Bowles, also made use of some of Conder's maps and was associated with Ebenezer Bourne and Benjamin Baker, both of whom later worked with Colonel Mudge on the early Ordnance Survey sheets.

Conder's map of Cambridgeshire carries the title of the map within a cartouche in the top right hand corner. Beneath, is a shield bearing the arms of the city of Cambridge and the scale is placed in the lower right hand corner. There is a table of symbols and beneath this, some way down the map, a compass indicator. Conder's name is printed outside the border of the map in the lower right hand corner. County boundaries are indicated by dotted lines, together with important roads shown by means of double-engraved lines. The extensive drainage system in the north of the county is engraved in similar fashion.

Several of Conder's smaller maps were engraved together on the same sheet of copper and when the maps are separated it is necessary to attach false margins to some of their edges as with this example.

Most of Conder's maps tend to be found in historical works rather than in atlases but they make an attractive addition to a collection. The works in which they appear have now become quite costly and are unlikely to be broken-up if they are in good condition. As a result the maps are becoming more expensive and difficult to find.

Size: $7\frac{3}{4}$ inches $\times$ $6\frac{3}{8}$ inches
    (198mm $\times$ 162mm)

Rating 3

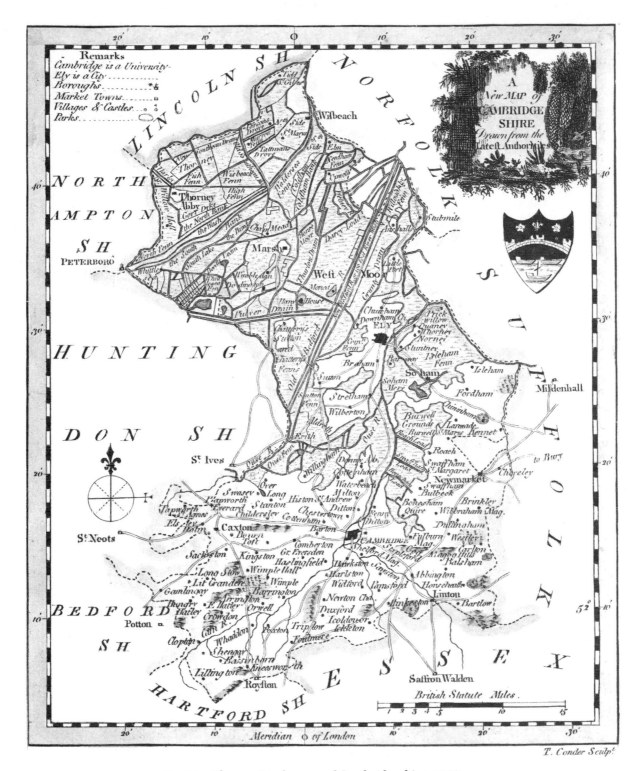

No. 37   Thomas Conder map of Cambridgeshire, 1786

John Tuke, fl.1786

In 1787 a fine four-sheet map of Yorkshire was published, engraved by John Tuke who also prepared this map of Holderness on a scale of $\frac{3}{4}$ inch to the mile, dated a year earlier. The map details this important part of the north-east coast and takes in the county town of Beverley and the important working port of Kingston-upon-Hull. The map is carefully engraved from a copper plate now in the writer's ownership. As mentioned elsewhere, the map is printed on fine Whatman paper bearing a date watermark of 1794.

Mr. R. Vere Tooley makes reference to changing coastlines brought about by erosion and accretions in his Introduction to *Maps and Map-Makers* (Batsford 1972). Writing about this particular coastal area he says:—"Spurn-head in Yorkshire, with its relatively modern accretions (Sunk Island, still showing in the 18th century, in the 19th is part of the mainland) ...". On the other hand, John Tuke records some of the losses. We see from the map "Hartburn washed away by the sea, Hyde, lost by the sea, Site of the town of Hornsea Beck and Site of the ancient church of Withernsea". These last two locations now appear about half a mile off-shore. The reader will note that the erosion is due to the German Ocean.

I acquired this map for reasons of sentiment having spent much of my youth happily afloat on this treacherous river.

Size: $24\frac{1}{8}$ inches × $18\frac{7}{8}$ inches
(613mm × 480mm)

Rating 2

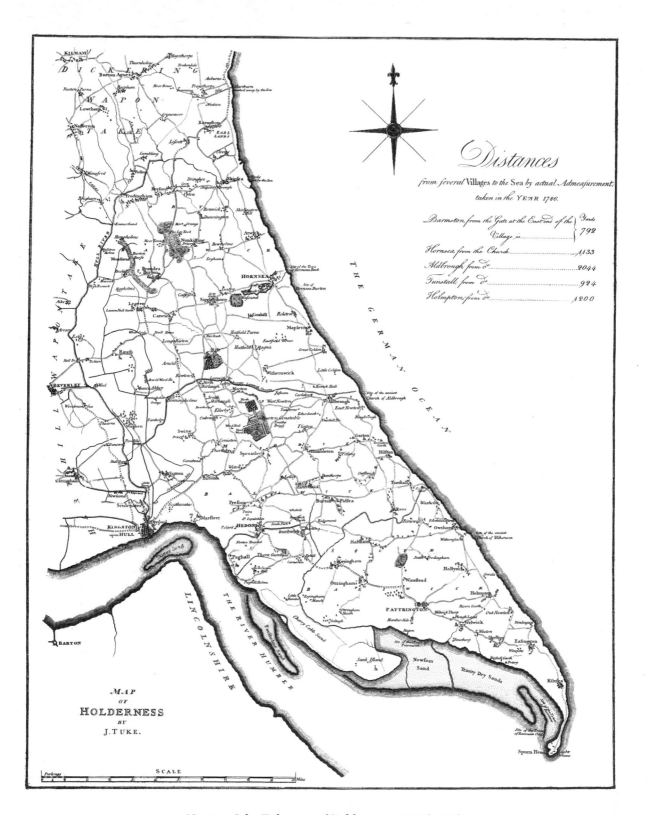

No. 38   John Tuke map of Holderness, 1786 (1794)

John Cary, c. 1754-1834

In 1759 the newly established Society of Arts offered an annual prize for an accurate survey of any English county on a scale of one inch to one mile. This gave an impetus to the production of large scale maps that lasted for something like fifty years. However, the difficulty with large scale maps is hanging space and apart from their display in public buildings there was little demand for them.

The up-dated information that went into their production provided a further link in the chain of development of British county mapping. Whilst the publishers of large scale maps were finding increasing difficulty in selling them, a new engraver and publisher, John Cary, started in 1787 to issue small atlases which were inexpensive and provided accurate up-dated information on the principal roads of the Kingdom.

Cary was so successful that in 1794 he was engaged by the Postmaster-General to undertake a survey of all the main roads of the country. An example from this atlas is illustrated and shows a departure from mapping on a county basis, a practice followed since Elizabethan times.

Cary's three important works likely to be sought by the collector are *Cary's Traveller's Companion* first published in 1789 containing miniature county maps ($3\frac{5}{8}$ inches by $4\frac{7}{8}$ inches); *Cary's New and Correct English Atlas* published in 1787, ($10\frac{1}{4}$ inches by $8\frac{1}{4}$ inches) and his larger *New English Atlas* published in 1809 (19 inches by 21 inches).

Most of Cary's county atlases were re-published many times and examples of his maps are not too difficult to obtain at the present time.

Size: $10\frac{1}{4}$ inches $\times$ $8\frac{1}{4}$ inches   Rating 3
    (260mm $\times$ 209mm)

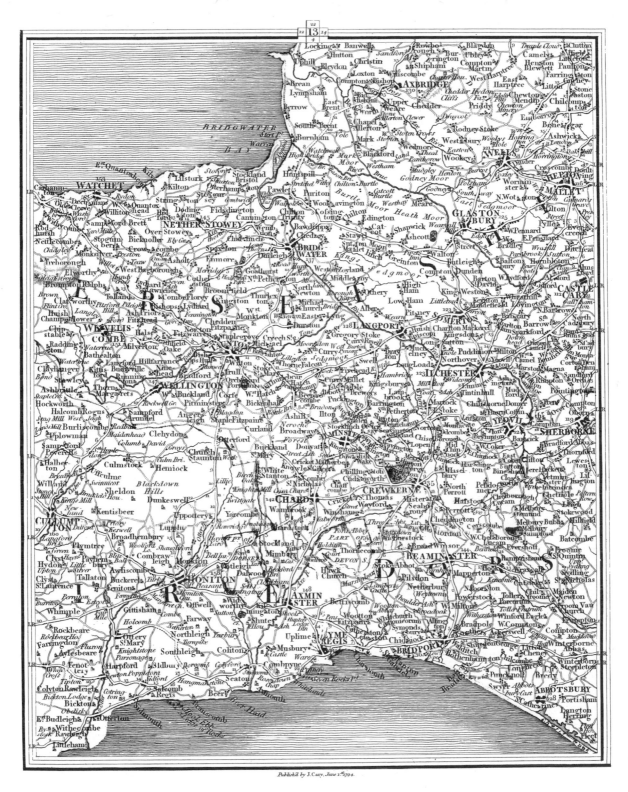

Published by J.Cary, June 2.ᵈ 1794.

No. 39   John Cary map of Somerset, Dorset and Devon (parts), 1794

Robert Laurie and James Whittle, c.1797

One of the great delights of collecting is the excitement of discovering a new 'find' especially when it represents something that neither you, nor your collector friends, have seen before.

A Plan of Fishguard Bay depicts the landing of a French invasion force on the 22nd February, 1797. It was published by Messrs. Laurie and Whittle in the following March, probably as a special issue. It details the various positions of the opposing forces from the 22nd February until the French surrender on the 24th. The paper of the map bears a 1794 watermark, apart from which little else is known about its origin.

The following account, taken from Dugdale's *England and Wales Delineated* turns the map into a piece of living history.

". . . on the 22nd February, 1797, a French force under General Tate landed at Goodwich-beach a few miles southward of the town. The force consisted of about 1,200 men, but without field pieces. It was pleasing to hear of the zeal with which the natives poured down from the mountains to resist this inroad. It appears that above 3,000 countrymen and miners assembled, armed with scythes, forks and other ready weapons, besides the militia and volunteers of Pembroke and Cardigan. Lord Cawdor took command, but not being a military man, he submitted to the directions of Captain Mansell, who put the little fort at Fishguard into a state of defence, and took such judicious positions as soon convinced the French that they had no choice but to lay down their arms . . . The only difficulty he found, was to restrain the impetuosity of the mountaineers, who fell upon the French without orders indeed, but with irresistable fury. Some few were killed by this irregular attack, but on the arrival of the militia and volunteers, the invaders surrendered prisioners of war . . .''

Size: $5\frac{1}{2}$ inches $\times$ $8\frac{3}{4}$ inches   Rating 1
     (140mm $\times$ 223mm)

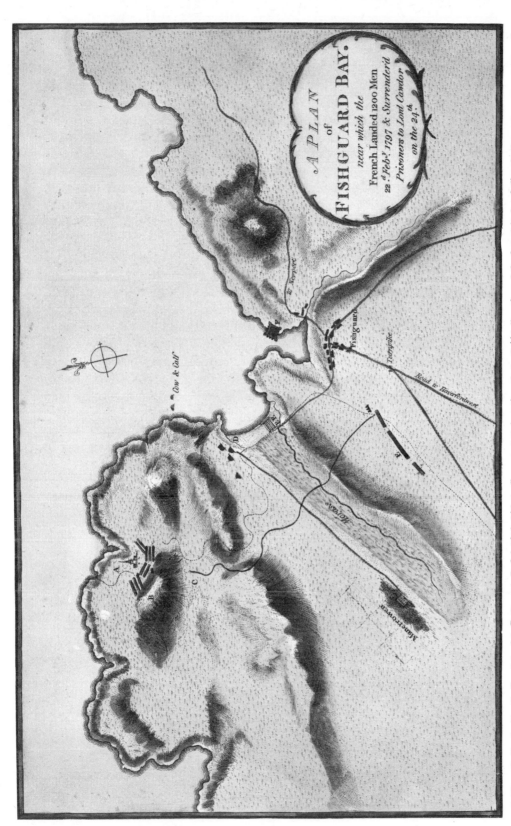

A PLAN of FISHGUARD BAY. near which the French Landed 1200 Men 22.d Feb.y 1797 & Surrenderd Prisoners to Lord Cawdor on the 24.th

A. Llanwnda Church where the French landed . B. Penanor Rocks behind which the Enemy took their station . C. the British line of march the first night, but finding the Enemy too numerous, returned to the Station R. B.B. the second days Position . F. Fishguard Fort .

§ The dotted Lines denote the march of the Enemy down to Goodwick Sands, where they piled their Arms, and surrendered themselves Prisoners .

The Red denotes the British Infantry , the Light Blue Lord Cawdors Horse, and the dark Blue the Yoeman . ⚟ Artillery on the right . D. Goodwick Village .

No. 40   Laurie and Whittle plan of Fishguard Bay, 1797

John Cary, c.1754-1834

We have previously looked at the work of John Cary (map No. 39) but that particular example, although important, is hardly representative in style and appearance of most of Cary's maps.

Many British atlases published in the eighteenth and early nineteenth century tended to confine themselves to the county maps of England. Frequently, Wales, Scotland and Ireland were either omitted or had to make do with regional maps like the one illustrated of the South Part of Scotland.

This was one of two general maps of Scotland that appeared in Cary's Atlas published by John Stockdale in 1805 with outline hand colour.

The county title is contained in a plain oval cartouche and there is a reference to the Shires and a grid, otherwise the map is without ornament and is typical of the accurate and functional format of Cary's work. This map is so modern in appearance that it hardly seems possible that it was produced nearly one hundred and eighty years ago. Because of this, the maps are rarely used for furnishing purposes and their interest and appeal lies with the serious collector. Similar examples are not difficult to find and they are relatively cheap to buy.

Size: $14\frac{7}{8}$ inches $\times$ $20\frac{1}{2}$ inches   Rating 4
      (378mm $\times$ 520mm)

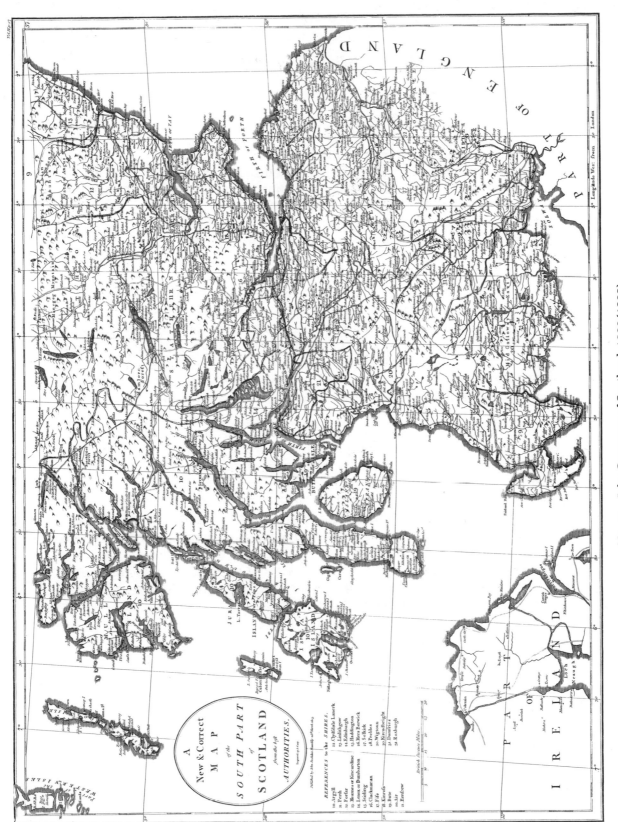

No. 41   John Cary map of Scotland, 1803 (1808)

John Luffman, fl.1775-1820

Map No. 42

In 1803, John Luffman, a London map-seller and engraver, of 28, Little Bell Alley, Coleman Street, published his *New Pocket Atlas and Geography of England and Wales*.

This tiny work contained fifty-four curious circular county maps of England and Wales, each measuring approximately one and three quarter inches in diameter. Beneath each is a type-set text giving details of the county, its size, number of towns and parishes, the number of houses and the population. Also included is information on the climate, industry and products, together with geographical details including rivers and the terrain.

Luffman is represented with his map of Merionethshire. Nine towns and villages are marked together with roads and the bordering counties of Carnarvon, Denbigh and Montgomeryshire. Within the circular border of the map appears the name of the county, the scale of miles (approximately one half inch to the mile) and the information that the county town is Harlech and is 225 miles from London, to which the county send one member of Parliament.

Near the outer circular border is the plate number nine. On a similar copy published in 1805/6 this plate number has been moved about half an inch away from the map. This is possibly a means of dating the editions. The map itself is line-engraved and the lower edge of the plate-mark is partially obscured by the first line of type below it.

Although maps from this Atlas are of comparatively recent origin they are extremely scarce and will prove difficult to find. An experienced collector friend is of the opinion that the Atlas was used for teaching geography in Georgian times. If this is so, there may still be households which possess the Atlas without appreciating its rarity and value. Again, because the Atlas is tiny, its mortality rate has been high, and copies rarely appear on the market.

Size: 2⅜ inches diameter
    (60mm)

Rating 2

MERIONETHSHIRE is 36 miles in length from north to south, and about 34 in breadth from east to west. It is divided into 6 hundreds, which contain 4 market towns, 37 parishes, 5980 houses; and the population amounts to 29,506.

The air is cold, but healthy. The whole county being mountainous, and well clothed with wood, exhibits to the eye all the peculiar scenery belonging to a wild and romantic country. The herbs on the mountains, and the fish in the lakes, are much the same with those of the Alps. The inhabitants apply themselves wholly to grazing, and making butter and cheese. Sheep, black cattle, goats, game, and fish, are very plenty. Among the peaks is Cader-Idris, one of the highest in Wales. The principal rivers are the Dee and the Dovy.

No. 42   John Luffman map of Merionethshire, 1803

Edward Mogg, fl.1808-1826

One of the finest small road atlases of the early nineteenth century was published by Edward Mogg, a London engraver and publisher with premises at 51 Charing Cross.

The Atlas contains two hundred and twenty-three strip maps, each tastefully hand coloured in what appears to be a contemporary hand. The work is supported by an extensive Index giving details of the country seats of the nobility and gentry and 'The Direct and Cross Roads'.

It is dedicated to His Royal Highness The Prince Regent and the beautifully engraved frontispiece reads "A Survey of the High Roads of England and Wales Planned on a scale of one Inch to a Mile. Including the Seats of the Nobility and Gentry and every object worthy of remark, whether situated on, or contiguous to the Road". The date of publication is recorded as June 2nd 1817, although a number of the individual maps are dated 1814 or 1815.

The counties covered by this volume include Kent, Surrey, Sussex, Hampshire, Wiltshire, Dorset, Somerset, Devon and Cornwall, with part of Buckinghamshire and Middlesex.

Our example depicts the road from London to Exeter, maps No. 135 and 136. Winterslow Hut shown on the former, was the scene of an attack on the horses of the Exeter Mailcoach, by a lion, later the subject of a sporting print by artist James Pollard.

This kind of Atlas would receive extensive use in the early days of the nineteenth century when the coaching era was at its height, although copies of the maps now appear to be scarce.

Size: 8 inches × 5½ inches   Rating 2
    (203mm × 140mm)

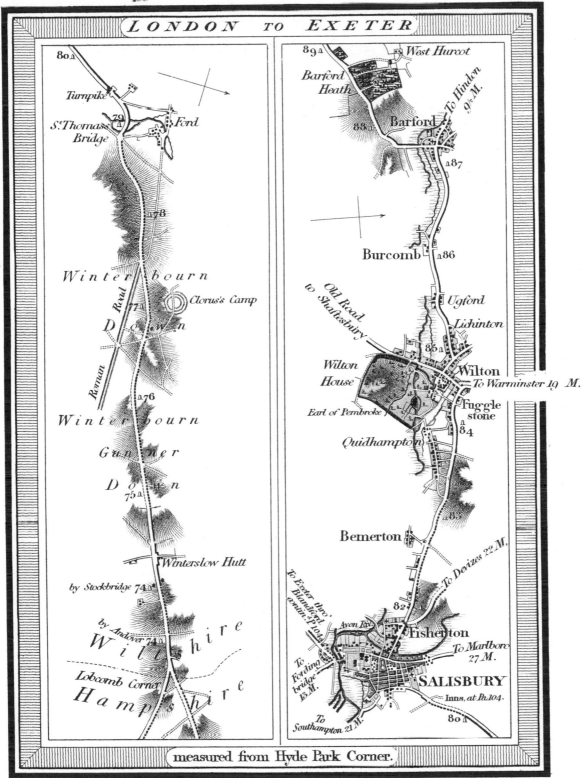

LONDON TO EXETER

80

Turnpike

79   S.T Thomas Bridge   Ford

78

Winterbourn

Read   77   Clorus's Camp

D o w n

Roman   76

Winterbourn

Gun ner

D o w n

75

Winterslow Hutt

by Stockbridge 74

by Andover 74

W i l t s h i r e

Lobcomb Corner

H a m p s h i r e

89   West Hurcot

Barford Heath

88   Barford   To Hindon 9½ M.

87

Burcomb   86

Old Road to Shaftesbury

Ugford

Lichinton

85

Wilton House   Wilton

To Warminster 19 M.

Earl of Pembroke   Fugglestone

84

Quidhampton

83

Bemerton

To Devizes 22 M.

To Exeter thro' Blandford, &c min. P.104

82

Avon Rivr   Fisherton

To Marlboro 27 M.

To Fording bridge 13 M.

SALISBURY

Inns, at Pa.104.

To Southampton 21 M.

80

No. 43   Edward Mogg road map London to Exeter (part), 1814

Langley and Belch, fl. 1800-1835

Map No. 44

Edward Langley was a competent engraver as well as senior partner in the London printing and publishing firm of Langley and Belch. In 1818 this firm produced a most attractive Atlas containing fifty-three maps of the counties of England and Wales, represented here by the map of Huntingdonshire.

The county title is positioned outside the ruled border at the top of the map and is inscribed *Langley's New Map of Huntingdonshire*. In the upper right hand corner is a list of the hundreds with a compass device and the key beneath.

An attractive vignette, a feature of this series of maps, is positioned in the lower left hand corner. It depicts the old church at St. Ives and in the foreground is a sailing barge with workmen loading (or unloading) cargo from a horse and cart. The four hundreds on the map are finely wash-coloured in a contemporary hand, a particular feature of maps in this series. Roads are well detailed and classified either as mail-coach or turnpike, with distances between towns given in large figures—smaller figures denote the towns' distance from London.

The Atlas was re-issued in 1821, but not again after that date. Copies of the maps are difficult to obtain, possibly because the original editions were not large. The series is interesting because it is one of the last to carry copper-plate engraved decorative features.

Size: 6¾ inches × 10 inches   Rating 2
(171mm × 254mm)

LANGLEY'S new MAP of HUNTINGDONSHIRE.

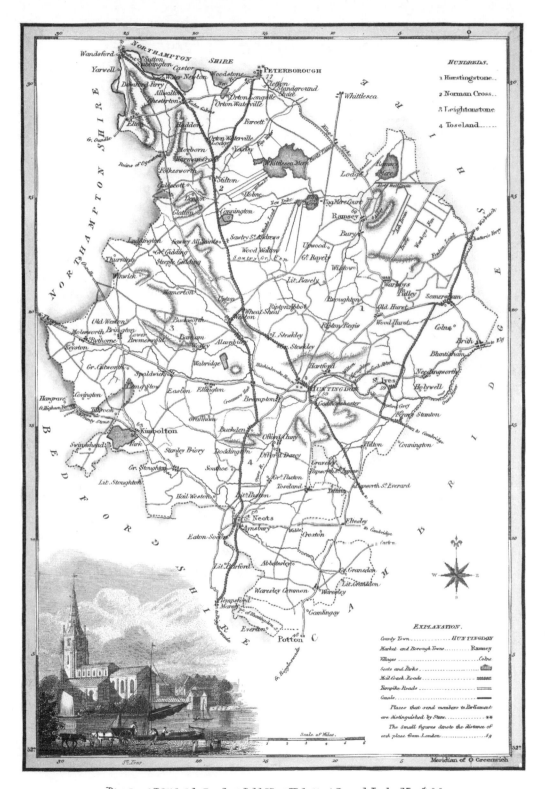

HUNDREDS.

1 Hurstingstone..
2 Norman Cross..
3 Leightonstone
4 Toseland ......

EXPLANATION.

County Town	HUNTINGDON
Market and Borough Towns	Ramsey
Villages	Colne
Seats and Parks	
Mail Coach Roads	
Turnpike Roads	
Canals	

Places that send members to Parliament are distinguished by Stars .... ⁑

The small figures denote the distance of each place from London 54

Scale of Miles.

Meridian of Greenwich

Printed and Published by Langley & Belch, No. 173, High Street, Borough, London, May 1st 1818.

No. 44   Langley and Belch map of Huntingdonshire, 1818

The Ordnance Survey

One of the most important reasons for needing an accurate map is in order to make war and the origins of our Ordnance Survey may be traced to the Jacobite rising in Scotland when Prince Charles at the head of his army reached as far south as Derby. After his subsequent defeat at Culloden, General Wade was ordered to open up the highlands by building military roads that would enable the rapid movement of troops from one part of the country to another. The mapping for the project was undertaken by William Roy who later became Surveyor-General of Coasts and Engineer for making Surveys under the Honourable Board of Ordnance.

In 1791 the offices of the Survey were established in the Tower of London along side those of the Ordnance and Colonel William Mudge became Director. The first county to be surveyed was Kent, published in January, 1801. The other southern counties followed and by the year 1844, surveys had been completed as far north as Hull in Yorkshire.

The map of the northern coastal region of Cardigan is reproduced from the survey sheet published by Colonel Mudge in 1819 as part of the first national survey of the country. The imprint, inscribed near the margin at the bottom of the map states "Engraved at the Drawing Room in the Tower under the Direction of Col. Mudge by Benjm. Baker and Assistants—The Writing by Ebenr. Bourne".

However, much of the later success of the Ordnance Survey was due to General Colby, who in 1824 established the 13th (Survey) Company, Royal Engineers.

These first editions of the Ordnance Survey are now collector's items and well worth including in a collection. They were engraved on copper plates and display all the fine qualities of the engraver's art.

Size: $24\frac{1}{2}$ inches $\times$ $36\frac{3}{8}$ inches
    (622mm $\times$ 924mm)

Rating 3

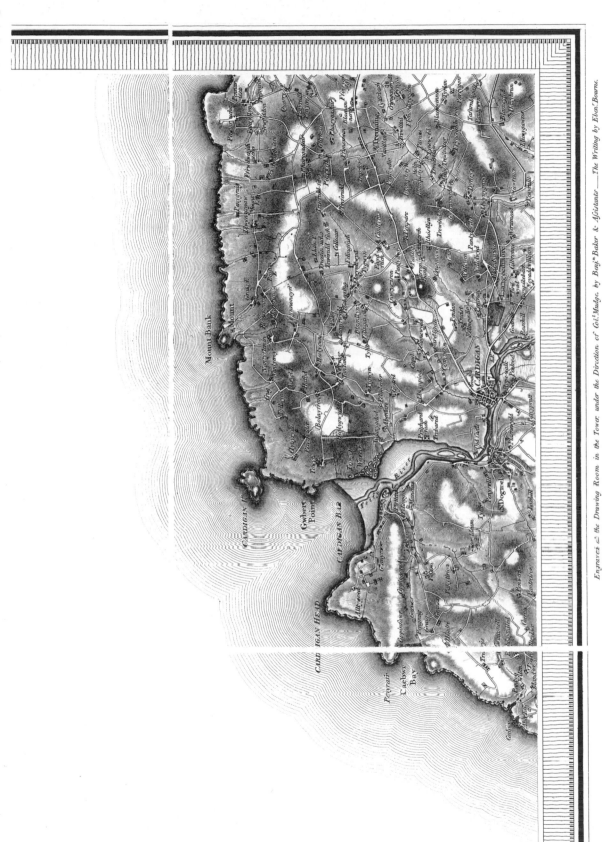

Engraved at the Drawing Room in the Tower under the Direction of Col.ᵉ Mudge, by Benj.ⁿ Baker & Assistants —The Writing by Ebenᵉ Bourne.

No. 45   Ordnance Survey map of Cardigan, 1819

William Darton, fl.1820

No book about the antique maps of Britain would be complete without a look at the work of William Darton.

This British publisher issued *A Complete Atlas of the English Counties* in 1822, containing forty-two folio maps, with further editions in 1830, 1833 and 1848. Despite the number of editions, the maps are not easy to find. The preamble to the first edition states that the maps were "Commenced by the late Thomas Dix, of North Walsham; carried on and completed by William Darton".

The maps are beautifully engraved on copper, hand coloured before issue, with full wash-colouring to the hundreds. Each had a pleasing vignette engraved in one of the corners. In the case of Buckingham the view is of Gray's Monument at Stoke Park.

The 'Explanation' in the upper right hand corner provides information on market towns with their distance from London, mail roads, principal roads, cross roads, canals, rivers, gentlemens seats, churches and chapels. Electoral information includes polling places and details of the number of members returned to Parliament. There is a reference to the hundreds and in the lower right hand corner, a compass indicator and scale.

This series is one of the last to incorporate decorative features and makes an attractive and relatively inexpensive addition to any home. They are, however, somewhat prone to ink transfer as frequently ink from the vignette transfers to the opposite side of the map.

Size: $17\frac{1}{4}$ inches × $14\frac{1}{4}$ inches   Rating 2/3
    (438mm × 362mm)

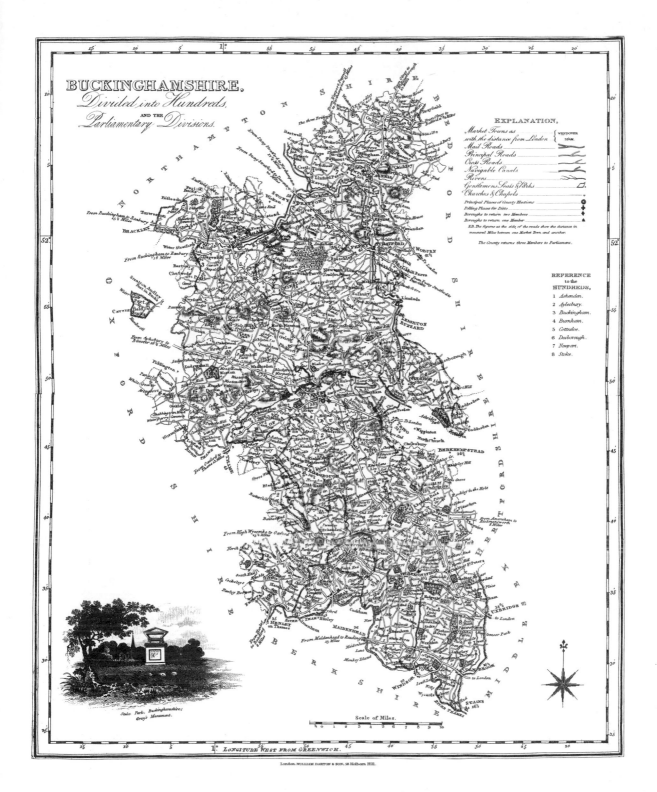

No. 46   William Darton map of Buckinghamshire, 1822 (1833)

Aristide Michel Perrot, 1793-1879

Map No. 47 (a) (b)

This charming set of miniature maps, often referred to as the 'gravestone series' due to the resemblance many of them bore to a grave headstone, were published in a six volume French work entitled *L'Angleterre ou Description Hist et Topographique du Royaume de la Grand Bretagne*. The author of the work was G. B. Deeping and the maps were based on the researches of French geographer Michel Perrot and engraved on copper plates by M. Migneret.

They carry the date 1823 after Perrot's signature although a further issue that same year and a subsequent one in 1835 are without dates. All are without borders and carry the name of both topographer and engraver.

The examples illustrated carry original outline hand-colour to the county boundaries and are possibly one of the most unusual series of miniature county maps ever published.

Example (a) depicts the old Scottish maritime counties of Aberdeen and Kincardine with the fishing and farming interests of the region depicted in the surrounding vignette. The County of York (b) includes the entire county together with its principal rivers and some of the more important towns. Maritime influence is represented by an anchor fluke and a fish, the woollen industry by a sock and manufacture by a jug and basin.

Maps from the series cover the British Isles and it is refreshing to find an early nineteenth century work with both Scotland and Ireland represented. Examples rarely appear on the market; the writer having looked in vain, for many years, for the one of Wiltshire.

Size approx: $4\frac{1}{4}$ inches × $2\frac{3}{4}$ inches   Rating 2
(108mm × 70mm)

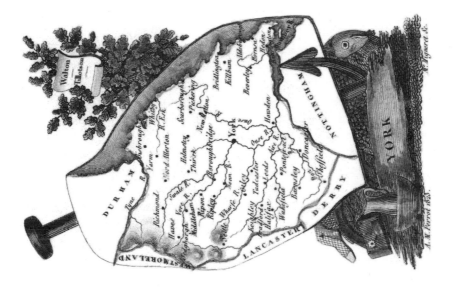

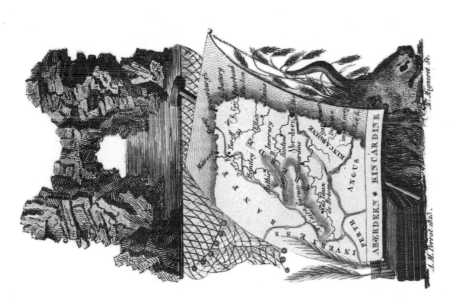

No. 47   Michel Perrot maps of a) Aberdeen and Kincardine, 1823. b) York, 1823

Henry Teesdale, fl.1840

One of the finest maps of South Wales to be published in the nineteenth century appeared in Henry Teesdale's *New British Atlas* in 1829.

My copy is printed on Whatman paper with the watermark J. Whatman Turkey Mill 1829, although it is likely that this particular map was a later issue, possibly between 1840 and 1848.

The engraved quality of the map is one of the best examples of nineteenth century work I have seen and the Atlas was probably hand coloured prior to issue. The hundreds are wash-coloured as is the sea, with the coastline heightened with additional colour. Mailcoach routes are coloured brown with the mileage marked between points along the routes, often at two mile intervals. Several railways are shown including the line from Brecon to Hay, the Carmarthenshire Railway and the Neath to Trecastle line.

There is an interesting link between Whatman the papermaker, mentioned earlier, and William Wynne Ryland, a Welsh engraver of outstanding ability. Ryland was a godson of the famous Welshman, Sir Watkin Williams Wynne, Bart., a patron of the Arts, to whom a number of eighteenth century Welsh maps and prints are dedicated.

Ryland was charged with forgery, a capital offence in those days. When Whatman was called to give evidence for the prosecution, he testified that the paper on which certain bonds had been engraved was made at his mill in Maidstone, but that mould marks in the paper indicated that it was made after the date on the bonds.

This evidence was so conclusive that Ryland was found guilty and sentenced to death. He was executed at Tyburn on the 29th August, 1783, the last offender to receive the death penalty for forgery in England.

There was a ready demand for the Teesdale Atlas and it continued to be published with a further eight editions over a period of twenty years until 1848, when it was taken over by Collins. Individual maps are fairly easy to obtain.

Size: $13\frac{1}{4}$ inches × $16\frac{1}{4}$ inches   Rating 4
    (337mm × 413mm)

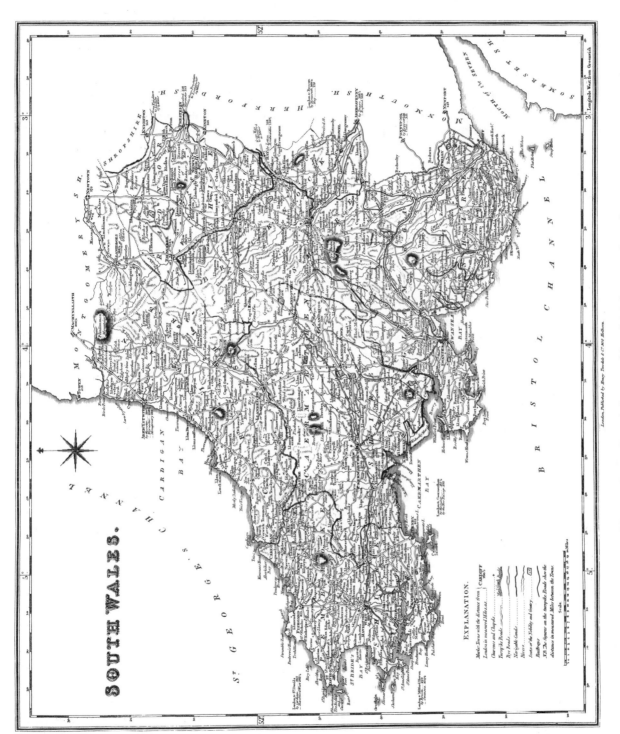

No. 48   Henry Teesdale map of South Wales, 1829 (1840)

James Pigot, fl.1830

In 1829, James Pigot and Company published a *British Atlas* containing forty-one maps of the counties of England, each tastefully hand-coloured in the traditional manner. The county title is incorporated in the upper printed border of the map. Other features include an attractive vignette relating to the county, together with a reference to the hundreds and information on the roads, rail-roads, rivers and canals.

Railway enthusiasts are reminded that references to 'rail-roads' on early issues of the maps does not relate to railways, but rather to the private tracks constructed by colliery and similar undertakings, where horse drawn trucks were employed. Railways started to appear on issues from 1838 onwards.

There were seven further issues of the Atlas between 1831 and 1844, and in 1846 its publication was taken over by Isaac Slater with a subsequent change of imprint.

It is worth mentioning that all the maps in this series were engraved on copper, one of the last to display decorative features. The supporting text is particularly interesting and ought to be supplied with the map at the time of purchase. In addition to details on the history of the county, there is information on soil, climate, produce and manufacture, rivers, canals and population, as well as an interesting distance table.

Despite the large numbers printed, certain of the more important counties are difficult to find.

Size: $13\frac{7}{8}$ inches × $8\frac{7}{8}$ inches   Rating 4
 (353mm × 226mm)

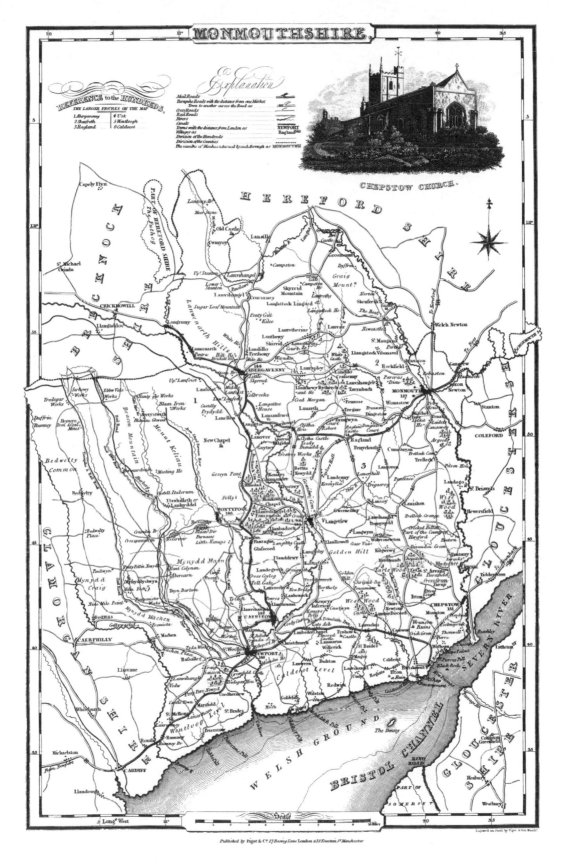

No. 49   Pigot & Co., map of Monmouth, 1829 (1831)

Christopher and John Greenwood, fl. 1820

One of the largest maps reviewed in this book is the one of Worcestershire, illustrated. This was published in an *Atlas of the Counties of England* issued in 1834 which contained forty-six maps. Each English county has a sheet to itself, but in the case of Wales several counties were grouped together. The title of the Atlas is, therefore, a little misleading. When I acquired a copy of some years ago, I was not expecting to find that it contained maps of Wales.

The Greenwoods were Yorkshiremen, Christopher (1786-1855) the elder of the two being the head of the firm of Greenwood and Company.

Their most important venture was a survey of England and Wales, followed by the publication of a series of large scale maps on a scale of one inch to the mile, issued between 1817 and 1830. The maps for the Atlas based on this series represent one of the most outstanding cartographic achievements of the nineteenth century.

The map has contemporary wash colouring to the hundreds and around the borders of surrounding counties. Hand colouring of a later date has been applied to the large engraving of Worcester Cathedral, located in the lower left hand corner. The map's title which embodies no less than five distinctive lettering styles, appears on the upper right hand portion of the map. In the upper left hand corner, an attractive compass device is positioned and the explanation or key, with seventeen sub-headings, is located in the bottom right hand corner.

A few years ago most map-dealers were not interested in selling maps from this series. "Too late and too large, unless you live in a castle" was the kind of comment that would meet an enquiry for a Greenwood map.

Most of the counties are still fairly easy to acquire.

Size: $23\frac{1}{4}$ inches × $26\frac{1}{2}$ inches   Rating 4
      (592mm × 673mm)

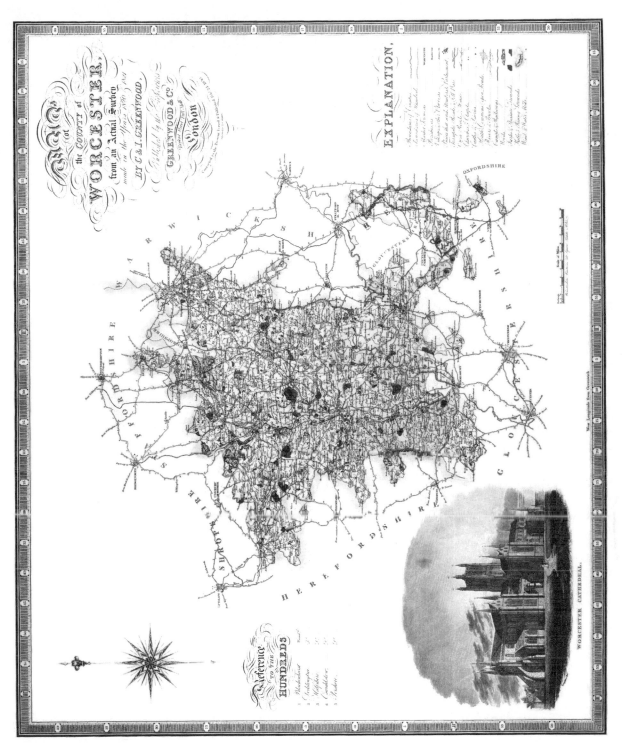

No. 50 John and Christopher Greenwood map of Worcestershire, 1830

Lt. Robert K. Dawson, R.E., c.1830

All the maps so far reviewed were made by line-engraving. There are a couple of exceptions—the map of Bath by Lt. Robert K. Dawson, R.E., and a curious map of North Wales which will be considered later. The technique used for the production of Lt. Dawson's map is known as lithography.

It was introduced by a German, Senefelder, about the year 1796 and involved drawing with a greasy pencil on the face of a specially prepared piece of limestone. The surface of the stone was then washed with an acid preparation which bit into the untreated area of the stone, after which water was allowed to soak into its surface. An inked roller was passed over the stone applying ink which adhered to the drawing, but not to the remainder of the stone's surface. Prints could then be taken from the drawing by applying pressure to the paper laid on the stone, providing the latter was kept moist and inked regularly. The process relied on the principle that grease and water do not mix.

The map of Bath comes from the boundary survey ordered by the Government of the day to implement the provisions contained in the Reform Bill of 1831. The Ordnance Survey, a branch of the Royal Corps of Sappers and Miners established in 1791 at the Tower of London, was already undertaking a national survey. In 1801 the first maps were printed covering the county of Kent, on the now familiar scale of one inch to one mile.

The work containing this map was completed between the years 1830-31 but the city had already been surveyed before that date, since Dawson's map carries the wording "From the Ordnance Survey".

The instructions to carry out the boundary survey were issued by Lord Melbourne to a Lt. Drummond, R.E., and are of sufficient interest to be quoted in part.

"... Sir,

His Majesty's Government being desirous to obtain and collect as much information as possible, and as speedily as my be consistent with accuracy, upon the different Cities and Boroughs included in Schedule (B) (C) and (D) of the Reform Bill, and also upon other Cities and Boroughs not included in any of the Schedules, but which are to retain the right of sending Members to Parliament, in order that when the Bill shall be passed into a Law, the Commissioners to be appointed under it may have the means of performing their duties with the

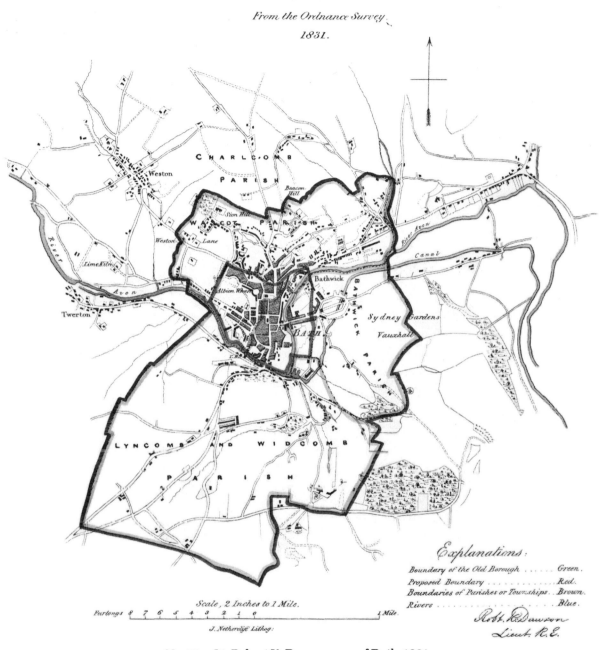

BATH.

From the Ordnance Survey
1831.

CHARLCOMB PARISH

WALCOT PARISH

Weston

Beacon Hill

Sion Hill

Weston Lane

LimeKiln

River Avon

Twerton

Albion Wharf

BATH

Bathwick

BATHWICK PARISH

Sydney Gardens

Vauxhall

River Avon

Canal

LYNCOMB AND WIDCOMB

PARISH

Explanations:

Boundary of the Old Borough . . . . . . Green.
Proposed Boundary . . . . Red.
Boundaries of Parishes or Townships . . Brown.
Rivers . . . . Blue.

Robt. K. Dawson
Lieut. R.E.

Scale, 2 Inches to 1 Mile.
Furlongs 8 7 6 5 4 3 2 1 0   1 Mile.

J. Netherclift Lithog:

No. 51   Lt. Robert K. Dawson map of Bath, 1831

137

greater expedition, I am to acquaint you that His Majesty's Government have seen fit to confide to you the superintendence of this Inquiry . . ."

Between August 1831 and January 1832 a copious work was compiled covering England and Wales. The surveys of Scotland and Ireland followed a few months later. They contain several hundred town plans and a great deal of information about population, number of houses, taxes and voting rights, together with census returns of males and females living in the various communities.

The plan of Bath is hand-coloured to differentiate between the existing borough boundary and the proposed one. It is drawn on a scale of two inches to one mile and carries a compass indicator and the signature of Lt. K. Dawson, R.E. Several lithographic printers were responsible for the production of the plans, J. Netherclift printing this example.

Although maps from the survey have little decorative merit, they are of considerable historical interest. I suspect the circulation of the survey was confined to local authorities and others affected by its findings. A copy is preserved in the House of Commons Library.

The maps are some of the earliest to be printed in the United Kingdom employing lithography. The use of stone for the printing surface was replaced by more sophisticated methods by the middle of the century.

Examples of the plans appear on the market quite often, but never it seems, the particular town one is looking for.

Size: $9\frac{1}{2}$ inches × $8\frac{1}{4}$ inches   Rating 3
    (242mm × 210mm)

John and Charles Walker, fl.1830

In 1833, Samuel Lewis published a *Topographical Dictionary of Wales* a two volume work containing maps of the counties of the Principality, together with a general map of Wales. This comprehensive work provides a fascinating history of the country and an account of industrial and commercial development during the Georgian period.

The Walker's are represented with their map of North and South Wales. The maps of the other eleven counties were also engraved by them.

The title, located off Cardigan Bay, displays the fine copper plate lettering style still in use at that time and claims the map shows the principal roads, rivers, railways and canals, but there were no commercial railways in Wales at this time. The 'railroad' shown as running from the Tredegar Iron Works to the coast east of Cardiff, was an industrial development that utilised 'horse power' for its locomotion. The map is a folding plate and appears at the front of the first volume.

The Walker brothers were publishers as well as prolific engravers. They produced their *British Atlas* in 1837 with reissues appearing almost annually until 1852. There were a further five between 1852 and the final one in 1879. Perhaps it should be mentioned that they also engraved the maps for Hobson's *Fox Hunting Atlas* which was overprinted with the names of the various hunts and the territory they covered. This was first published in 1850 and there were re-issues in 1866, 1868, 1870, 1872 and 1880.

The map of Wales commands a higher price than those of the individual counties and they are inexpensive and not difficult to find.

Size: $12\frac{1}{4}$ inches $\times$ $8\frac{7}{8}$ inches   Rating 5
    (312mm $\times$ 225mm)

No. 52   John and Charles Walker map of North and South Wales, 1832

Thomas Moule, 1754-1851

Late in the reign of William IV, Thomas Moule prepared a highly decorative set of maps of the English Counties, which were subsequently engraved on steel plates. Moule was a scholar, antiquarian and an authority on Heraldry so it is not surprising that he embellished his maps with armorials and other features. This was the last series of British maps to follow the tradition of decorative armorial cartography and they make a pleasing and attractive addition to any home.

Moule's map of the Isle of Man is possibly one of the most pleasing of the series. It is flanked on either hand by stone pinnacles, one containing a knight in armour, the other a bowman. The pinnacles support an ornate stone tracery which carries at its centre the armorial ensign of the Isle of Man—a device which dates from the time of Edward I. In this particular instance one may conclude that the arms of Man are legs! A crowned female figure holding a harp and spear, with a penant bearing the word 'Mona' (the Island's ancient name) is seated in the lower left hand corner. The map is orientated with west, instead of north to the top, a variation doubtless designed to help its presentation. Maps of the Island are uncommon and John Speed's Atlas is thought to have been the first to carry an example.

This map appeared in the fifth issue of the atlas published in 1842-3. The same plates were used for subsequent editions with the railways added. As railways do not appear on the first edition, dating the maps is easier. The title of the original work was *The English Counties Delineated* and there were issues in 1837, 1838 and 1841. In the 1842-3 edition, the title of the work was changed to *Barclay's Complete and Universal Dictionary* with subsequent printings in 1848, 1850 and 1852.

These particular maps appear to have been under-valued for years, dealers claiming they were too recent in origin to be of value. The fine quality of the engraved detail and their attractive composition has at last been recognised.

A number of publishers have issued reproductions, printing them in black and white and then hand-colouring them in the traditional manner. There is no information to indicate that they are reproductions. I have seen a number in antique shops which purport to be genuine. This could be ignorance on the part of the dealers concerned who may have bought in good faith. The reproductions are easy to detect providing an original is available for comparison. They are reproduced by a photo-

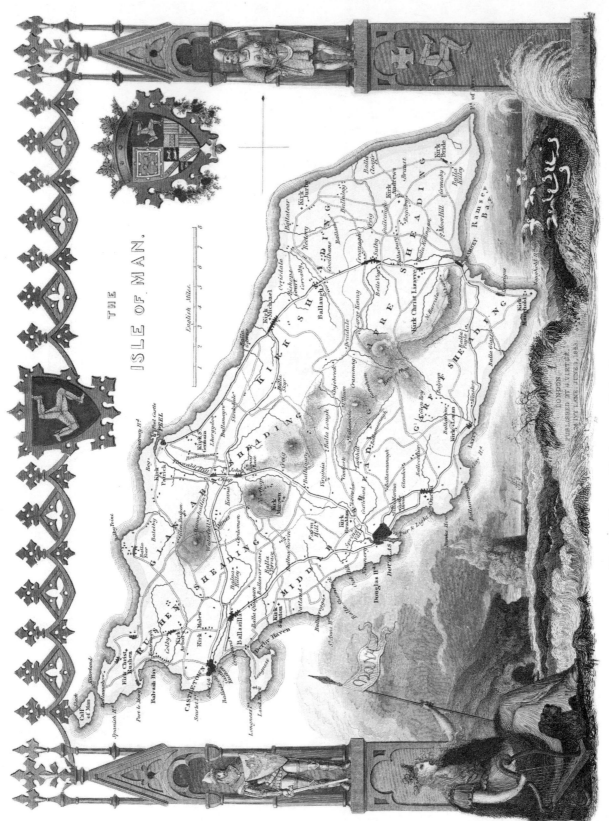

THE
ISLE OF MAN.

English Miles.

KIRK'S SHEADING
AYRE SHEADING
GARFF SHEADING
GLANFABA SHEADING
RUSHEN SHEADING
MIDDLE SHEADING

No. 53   Thomas Moule map of Isle of Man, 1836 (1843)

lithographic process (as our illustrations) and the fine engraving that appears in the sky on some of the little vignettes has a 'fuzzy' appearance when viewed through a magnifying glass, whereas originals display fine, sharp lines.

Size: $7\frac{3}{8}$ inches × $10\frac{1}{4}$ inches   Rating 4
      (188mm × 261mm)

Archibald Fullerton and Co.

Map No. 54

The last series of nineteenth century maps to carry decorative features were those of Fullerton and Co., published from 1840 onwards. These are carefully engraved on copper, each with an attractive vignette view relating to the county.

On the map of Devonshire illustrated there is an inset view of Exeter Cathedral. In the upper right hand corner is a table of the hundreds. The scale, with a compass indicator is positioned in the lower left hand. The maps carry interesting early detail on the railways, in this instance a section of the Exeter and Bristol Railway.

There were various issues of the Atlas in 1843, 1845, 1846 and 1848 and certain variations, including one with lithographed views.

A few years ago maps from the series were quite common and readily bought for two or three pounds. Whilst it is still possible to buy other small maps of the nineteenth century for a few pounds each, the decorative appeal of the Fullerton's has created a greater demand with a resulting rise in price.

This publisher produced an interesting world atlas of similar format, but this is beyond the scope of this book.

Size: $7\frac{1}{4}$ inches $\times$ $9\frac{3}{8}$ inches
(184mm $\times$ 238mm)

Rating 3

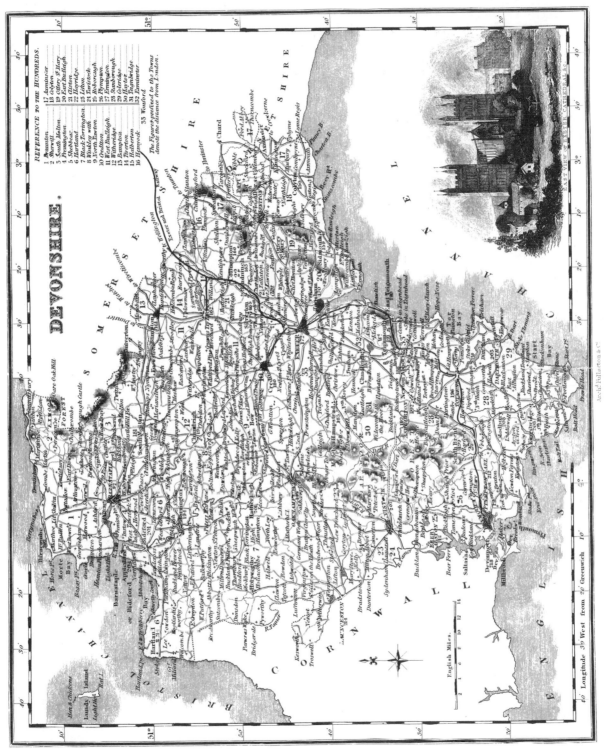

DEVONSHIRE.

No. 54   Archibald Fullerton & Co., map of Devonshire, 1843

Hugh Hughes, c.1845

This rare and unusual map of North Wales was printed by lithography, the same process used for the town plan of Bath, described earlier—map no. 51. Its title is *Dame Venodotia alias Modryb Gwen* (aunty Gwen). It was drawn on stone by Victorian landscape artist J. J. Dodd, R.A., from a design prepared by Hugh Hughes. The map was published by H. Humphreys of Castle Square, Carnarvon in about 1845.

It represents a map of North Wales in the shape of an old woman carrying a sack on her back. Hidden in her garments are many of the wild animals of Wales and behind her head, the peninsular running out to Great Orme's Head forms the head and shoulders of a young lady in a ball gown. Beneath the title, a key provides information on the region's towns, lakes, rivers, mountains and light-houses. The lettering below the map is a little indistinct, possibly due to a 'home grown' stone having been used. Although British limestone was used in the early days of lithography, it was rather coarse in texture and was later replaced by a fine-grained Dolomite limestone, especially imported for the purpose.

This new printing technique was capable of providing a great many copies without loss of quality. However, after a customer took delivery of an order, the drawing was usually erased from the stone which was re-used for the next illustration. Unlike a copper or steel printing plate, the work could not be printed again without a new drawing being prepared, a skilful and costly operation.

By the middle of the nineteenth century, lithography had established itself as a cheaper and speedier alternative to copper and steel plate printing, with their reliance on handmade plates. Before the century closed many illustrations, including maps, were being printed by means of this new technique. The camera was then combined with the process and photo-lithography was introduced. Within a few years of this development, thousands of engravers were thrown out of work and a skilled craft which had been practised since the fifteenth century disappeared almost overnight.

This map is rare and likely to be very difficult to acquire.

Size: $8\frac{5}{8}$ inches × $9\frac{1}{8}$ inches   Rating 1
    (218mm × 232mm)

Designed by H Hughes, and Drawn on Stone by J.J.Dodd.

DAME VENODOTIA, ALIAS MODRYB GWEN;
A Map of North Wales.

LAKES.	ANGLESEY.	CARNARVONSHIRE.	MERIONETHSHIRE.	FLINTSHIRE.	DENBIGHSHIRE.	MONTGOMERYSHIRE.	RIVERS.
1. Llanberis	8. Amlwch	20. Conway	34. Bestnog	53. Rhyl	62. Abergele	70. Llanidloes	A. Mersey
2. Nantlle	9. Llanerchymedd	21. Bangor	35. Maentwrog	54. Rhuddlan	63. Denbigh	71. Llanimr	B. Dee
3. Cywellyn	10. Holyhead	22. Aber	36. Harlech	55. St Asaph	64. Ruthin	72. Welshpool	C. Conway
4. Dinas	11. Gwalchmai	23. Carnarvon	37. Corwen	56. Flint	65. Wrexham	73. Machynlleth	D. Elwy
5. Capel Curig	12. Mona inn	24. Clynog	38. Trawsfynydd	57. Holywell	66. Llanrwst	74. Montgomery	E. Maewddach
6. Ogwen	13. Llangefni	25. Pwllheli	39. Bala	58. Caerwys	67. Chirk	75. Newtown	F. Dyfi
7. Cwmant	14. Beaumaris	26. Bethgelert	40. Barmouth	59. Hawarden	68. Llangollen	76. (Ch. Stretton)	MOUNTAINS.
8. Gwerngradd	15. Pentraeth	27. Bettws y coed	41. Dolgelley	60. Mold	69. Oswestry	77. (Bishops Castle)	G. Gt Ormeshead
9. Conway	16. Menai Bridge	28. Nevin	42. Dinas Mowddwy	61. Bangor		LIGHT HOUSES.	H. Penmaen mawr
10. Aled	17. Aberffraw	29. Porthdynllaen	43. Mallwyd	CARDIGANSHIRE.	ENGLISH TOWNS.	1. Bardsey	I. Snowdon
11. Elwern	18. Newborough	30. Tremadoc	44. Tabyn y gwrid	47. Machynros	50. Liverpool	2. South Stack	K. Mognant
12. Bala	19. Malltraeth	31. Port Madoc	45. Towyn	48. Borth	51. Parkgate	3. Skerries	N. Berwyn
13. Padyllyn		32. Hellheli	46. Aberdovey	49. Aberystwith	52. Chester	4. Point of Air	O. Cader Idris
		33. Crwceth			71. Shrewsbury	5. Leasowe	P. Plinlimon
						6. Black Rock	

PUBLISHED BY H HUMPHREYS, CASTLE SQUARE, CARNARVON

No. 55   Hugh Hughes map of North Wales, 1845

Reuben Ramble, fl. 1845

Reuben Ramble's delightful little school atlas *Travels through the Counties of England* was published in 1845 containing forty maps of the English counties. Each is surrounded by a series of vignette views relating to the particular county, although the maps themselves first appeared in Millers *New Miniature Atlas* in 1810.

In the case of Oxfordshire illustrated, the views include the City of Oxford, St. Mary's Church, Blenheim Palace, the Radcliffe Library and Christ Church. The maps are lithographed and would appear to have been hand coloured at the time of issue. Each map measures approximately $4\frac{1}{4}$ inches by $2\frac{3}{4}$ inches and is complete with scale and compass indicator. Railways are indicated by means of a dotted line and the map's margins carry graduations in latitude and longitude.

There is supporting text giving a description of the county set in quite a large type face, doubtless to facilitate easy reading by the young.

The Atlas was not issued again after 1845 and copies of the individual maps are costly and difficult to obtain.

Size: $4\frac{1}{4}$ inches × $2\frac{3}{4}$ inches (11 inches × 13 inches overall)   Rating 2
   (108mm × 69mm)

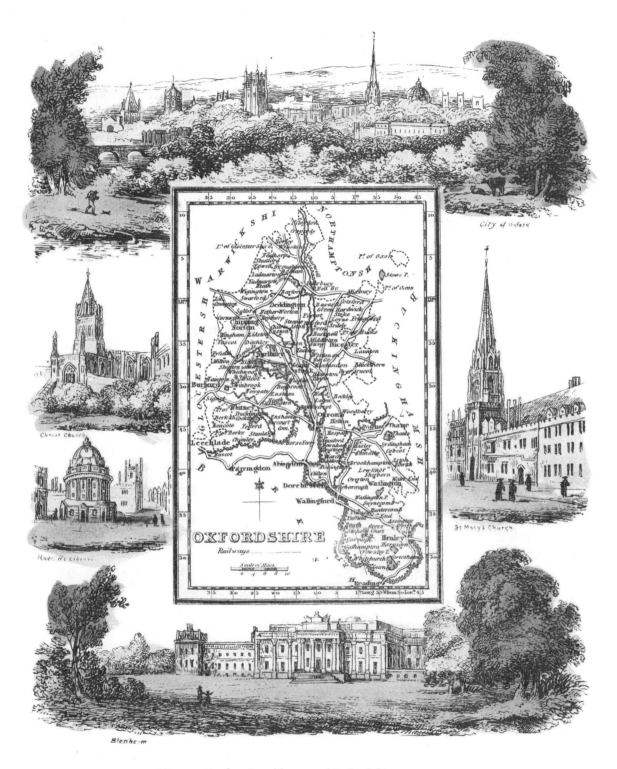

No. 56   Reuben Ramble map of Oxfordshire, 1845

John Archer, fl.1840

In 1835, Thomas Dugdale published *Curiosities of Great Britain and Ireland* an alphabetical, topographical dictionary containing a series of county maps by G. Cole and J. Roper. This work contains an interesting and extensive historical account of Britain. It was issued again in 1843 and 1848 and for the latter edition, the maps of Cole and Roper were replaced by a new series prepared and engraved by John Archer. There were further printings between 1854 and 1860.

Archer's map of Cornwall is made from a steel engraved plate. The discovery that printing plates could be made from steel, in preference to copper, was one of the major printing advances of the nineteenth century. It enabled illustrated editions of several thousand copies to be printed, whereas earlier copper plate editions had been confined to a few hundred.

This is typical work of a new generation of cartographers whose maps were plain, functional and accurate without the decoration or embellishment of previous centuries. Roads and railways were now recorded on maps with figures beneath the principal towns to denote their distance from London.

The 'rail-roads' that appear in the vicinity of Redruth used horses to pull the trucks of ore from the mines to both the north and south coast for shipment. Writing of Helston, Dugdale comments "The town, consisting of four streets, is well built and lighted with gas; in the centre formed by the intersection of the streets, stand the town-hall and market-house. This is one of the ancient stannary towns although little tin is now stamped here and the old coinage hall is inhabited as a private dwelling".

Maps of Cornwall are in great demand and one would have to pay several hundred pounds for a good, early example. Nevertheless, the output of atlases in Victorian times was considerable and examples like the one illustrated are still quite cheap to buy and fairly easy to find.

Size: 7 inches × 9¼ inches
(178mm × 235mm)

Rating 5

CORNWALL.

Drawn & Engraved by J.Archer,Pentonville,London.

SCALE

HUNDREDS

Stratton 1
Lesnewth 2
East 3
West 4
Trigg 5
Pyder 6
Powder 7
Kerrier 8
Penwith 9

SCILLY ISLES

St Helens I.   St Martins I.
Tresco I.   No Eastern Is.
Bryher I.   St Agnes I.
Hugh Town   St Marys I.
Annet
Crebawethan   St Agnes I.
Rosevean   Corregan.

D E V O N S H I R E

‡ Tavistock
207

Holsworthy
‡ 214

PLESTON

Plymouth
Plymouth Sound
Devonport

Camelford
228

B R I S T O L   C H A N N E L

E N G L I S H   C H A N N E L

St Ives Bay

Mounts Bay

Lands End Sennen

Lizard Pt.

West of 3° Greenwich

EXPLANATION

County Town .... BODMIN   Rail Roads
Market Towns .... Falmouth   Turnpike Roads
Villages,Hamlets &c. ... Newport   Cross Roads
Seats & Parks .... ▭   Boundary of Boroughs
Canals .... Ditto   Hundreds.
Polling Places .... ＋ Ditto   County.
Figures attached to Towns denote the distance from London.
Proposed Rail Roads

No. 57   John Archer map of Cornwall, 1848

John Tallis, fl. 1850

In 1850 John Tallis, a London publisher, issued a highly decorative world Atlas containing eighty maps engraved by J. Rapkin. The maps are finely engraved and surrounded by charming vignettes depicting famous landmarks, buildings and the dress and costume of the people of the country concerned. They appear to have been hand-coloured before issue, limited to outline colouring around the country. The vignettes were left uncoloured although many dealers now colour these to improve their decorative quality. The Atlas was issued several times during the early eighteen-fifties and some maps of the Crimea were later re-printed in historical works dealing with the War, by the London Printing and Publishing Company.

The map of Ireland is typical of maps in the series although I have chosen to include two maps of the Eastern and Western Hemispheres in my collection. The Western Hemisphere is a superb piece of balanced engraving; the vignettes include Eskimos, North and South American Indians and animals of the regions, including a polar bear, walrus, whales and penguins.

I recollect purchasing a copy of the atlas some six or seven years ago for thirty five pounds but I have recently seen copies carrying a price tag of nine hundred pounds. The maps of Australia and America are now very expensive and difficult to find and certain European countries including Holland, Germany (Prussia) and Switzerland are also in great demand.

There is a general map of Britain in the Atlas and this, together with the one of Ireland already mentioned somewhat limits the field as far as maps of the British Isles are concerned.

Size: 9 inches × 12 inches
    (228mm × 305mm)

Rating 3

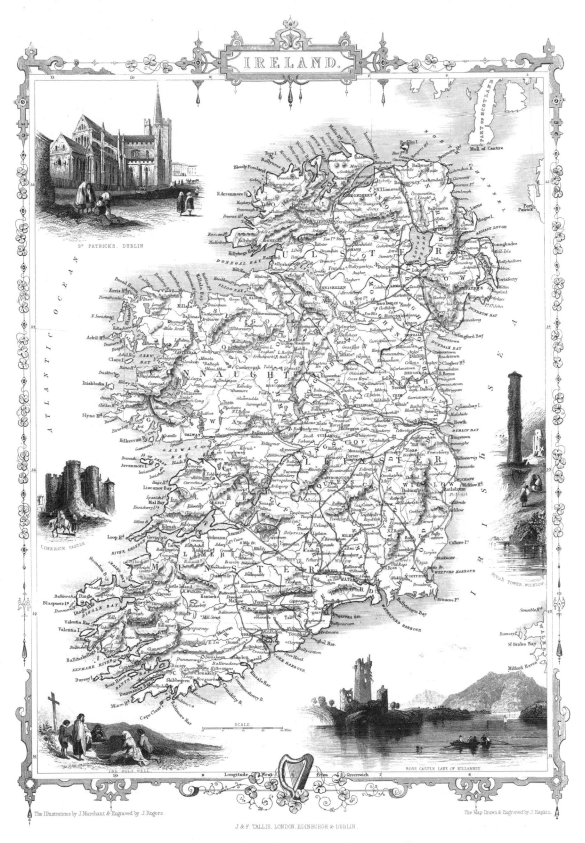

No. 58   John Tallis map of Ireland, c. 1850

Caricature Map of Wales

We conclude our look at three hundred years of British map-making with this unusual map of Wales which appeared in a children's book entitled *Geographical Fun*, a humourous outline of various countries. The book is inscribed 'A present from the Isle of Man'. It was published by James Blackwood and Company, and Hodder and Stoughton around 1869, price five shillings.

The map depicts Wales in the shape of Owen Glendowr wearing a crown and robe. It is printed in colours by lithography from the press of Vincent Brooks, Day and Son, successors to our earliest and most important firm of British lithographic printers and publishers, Messrs. Day and Haghe.

The type set verse beneath the map commences with the words 'Geography bewitch'd' a title used by Messrs. Bowles and Carver for a similar series of maps published in 1795, almost a century earlier. The text states that the drawings for the twelve maps were originally prepared by 'Aleph', a young lady, aged fifteen. They were intended to help the recovery of her younger brother who was ill in bed, by keeping him amused and adding to his geographical knowledge. The idea for the maps is stated to have been taken from an illustration of Mr. Punch riding on a dolphin in the shape of England and Wales.

The Atlas contains twelve maps; England, Wales, Scotland, Ireland, Holland with Belgium, Denmark, Russia, France, Spain, Italy, Prussia and Germany.

An interesting booklet, *Cartographical Curiosities* published by British Museum Publications (1978) provides a number of illustrations of similar maps, including Dame Venodotia (see No. 55). Examples from the series are uncommon and likely to be difficult to find.

Size: $7\frac{7}{8}$ inches $\times$ $9\frac{1}{2}$ inches   Rating 2
(200mm $\times$ 241mm)

CENTRAL LIBRARY, MARKET SQUARE, PRESTON 53191

WALES.

Geography bewitch'd—Owen Glendowr,
In Bardic grandeur, looks from shore to shore,
And sings King Arthur's long, long pedigree,
And cheese and leeks, and knights of high degree.

No. 59   Caricature map of Wales — Vincent Brooks, Day & Son, c. 1870

Useful Books

Antique Maps of Wales, John Booth. Cambridge House Books, (1978). A look at some of the maps of Wales published between 1573-1860.

Antique Maps by P. J. Radford. Garnstone Press, (1970). An inexpensive guide for the beginner to collecting, covering both United Kingdom and foreign maps and map-makers.

County Atlases of the British Isles (1579-1703) by R. A. Skelton. Carta Press, (1970). An excellent bibliography for the serious collector by a leading authority.

Discovering Antique Maps by A. G. Hodgkiss. Shire Publications. Remarkable value at 50p. A detailed and easily read introduction to the subject; illustrated.

How to Identify Old Maps and Globes by Raymond Lister. G. Bell and Sons, (1965). A most informative work with an excellent bibliography and an interesting section on old watermarks.

Investing in Maps by Roger Baynton-Williams. Corgi Books, (1971). Possibly the best topical work on the subject by a leading authority. Excellent illustrations with interesting text.

Les Filigranes by C. M. Briquet. Watermarks to 1600, (1907). The standard work on this subject.

London Map-Sellers 1660-1720 by Sarah Tyacke. Map Collector Publications Ltd., 1978. A detailed and interesting study of the London map-trade, its personalities and their trading practices.

Maps and Map-Makers by R. V. Tooley. Batsford 1970. A look at the world's cartographic development in a single volume. A fine reference work.

Watermarks in Paper in Holland, England, France, etc., in the XVII and XVIII Centuries W. A. Churchill (1935). A useful guide to watermarks and paper-makers.

Watermarks Mainly of the 17th and 18th Centuries. Edward Heawood. (1950). A well detailed study. Includes marks on the earlier maps of Britain and the Continent.

157

Glossary

ARMORIAL
Usually a shield-like device bearing the coat-of-arms of a nobleman.

ANTIQUE MAP
An impression taken from a hand-made printing plate, printed at least 100 years ago.

BURIN
An engraving tool.

CALLIGRAPHY
The various lettering styles.

CAMEO OR RELIEF PRINTING
Printing from a raised printing surface, e.g. woodcuts or lithographs.

CARTOGRAPHER OR COSMOGRAPHER
A map-maker

CARTOUCHÉ
An ornamental device usually surrounding the name of the map, scale of miles etc. Often incorporates scrolls, strapwork, figures, (cherubs were very popular) fruit, garlands, flowers and the like.

DELINEAVIT, DESCRIPSIT, DEL.
(he drew it) May follow the originator's name on the map or print.

"d"
Died.

ETCHING
Use of acid to 'bite' a plate instead of a graver (the tool used by an engraver).

FECIT
Latin translation (he did it) may follow engraver's name on a map or print.

fl.
flourished.

FOXING
Discolouration on a map or print caused by damp, or the mineral impurities in the paper.

GRAVER
Sharp pointed tool used for engraving.

HYDROGRAPHER
Maker of Marine Charts.

HUNDRED
Defined local area on a county map, dating from the 11th century—a unit of administration between parish and shire. Northern term was Wapentake (Danish) or ward. In Kent the hundreds were known as Lathes.

INTAGLIO
Pronounced *In-tal-i-o*, an incised printing surface.

IMPRESSION
A copy taken on paper or other suitable material from a printing plate.

ILLUMINEUR
A map colourist

LINE-ENGRAVING
A hand process of incising a copper or steel plate in order to produce a design for printing purposes.

LAID DOWN
Indicates that a map or a print has been stuck to a card or other suitable backing. Damaged items were often "Laid down".

PLATE-MARK
An incised line around the border of a map or print caused by the pressure of the press on the printing plate.

REPRODUCTION OR REPROGRAPHIC
A copy of a map or illustration usually made by a photo-lithographic process.

RE-PRINT
A subsequent impression taken from a printing plate after the original issue.

RE-STRIKE
A modern impression taken from an old printing plate.

STATE
Refers to the condition of the printing plate. The plate in original printing condition is its first state. Any additional *engraved* work on the plate for a subsequent printing would make the plate second state, and so on. Alterations to the plate determined its state, not the number of copies printed from it.

SCULPSIT, Sc., SCULP INCIDENTE
The engraver and often follows his name on a map or print.

WATERMARK
A device incorporated into the paper at the time of manufacture, normally visible when the paper is held to the light. Can be helpful in dating manuscripts or maps.

Index

Index (continued)

Index (continued)

Index (continued)

Index (continued)